Australia's Finest
GOLF COURSES

Darius Oliver

Principal photographer David Scaletti
Foreword by Ian Baker-Finch

NEW
HOLLAND

CONTENTS

NEW SOUTH WALES AND THE AUSTRALIAN CAPITAL TERRITORY

WESTERN AUSTRALIA

QUEENSLAND

SOUTH AUSTRALIA

FOREWORD

As a player, designer and golf analyst I have had the good fortune of being able to travel the world playing the game I love on some of the finest courses in existence. I always look forward to returning home to Australia and playing all the great golf courses both old and new.

Internationally the Australian game is extremely well regarded with an enviable record in major tournaments and a host of home-grown champion golfers continuing to successfully ply their craft on the toughest tours abroad. For decades we have also enjoyed a reputation for having some of the best golf per capita in the world. While I wouldn't dare disagree with this sentiment, it could be argued that the perception is based on the quality of a handful of celebrated classics such as Kingston Heath, Royal Melbourne and many of the Sandbelt-based courses in Victoria. Along with The Lakes, The Australian, Royal Sydney, New South Wales, Lake Karrinyup, Royal Queensland and Royal Adelaide, these are the courses that every travelling golfer deliberately seeks out, and rightfully so.

Thankfully the long period of quality golf design inactivity between the golden era of the 1920s and the boom days of the 1980s is well and truly behind us, and the industry is again producing world-class golf experiences.

Until recently it appeared that all our great golf land was taken; now it seems great courses on great sites are popping up everywhere. I'm delighted that the landscape has changed and proud to have been personally involved with Michael Coate and Roger Mackay in the design and construction of such a course at Kennedy Bay in Perth, which I believe is one of the finest links style courses in the country. Another new course, designed by Greg Norman and Bob Harrison—the Moonah Course at The National on the Mornington Peninsula, south of Melbourne—will certainly become one of the 'must play' destinations in Australian golf.

The spectacular courses from the MacKenzie era, such as Royal Melbourne and Kingston Heath, with the benefit of more than 70 years to grow and mature, remain our most distinguished. The exciting prospect for golfers throughout the country today though is the genuine quality of a number of the newcomers. This modern era has enhanced the standard of the game and confirmed the oft-held belief that Australia is truly one of the great destinations in world golf, especially given the relatively low cost of green fees by world standards.

So whether you are a private or public golfer, beginner, professional, social player or absolute aficionado I'm certain you will enjoy this superbly presented tour through the very best golf courses our wonderful country has to offer.

Ian Baker-Finch

*Pelican Waters
2nd hole.*

INTRODUCTION

Like a generation of Australian golfers, I grew up with Greg Norman posters on the wall and Tom Ramsey golf books by the bed. While Norman's style and charisma captivated and inspired thousands to take up the game, Ramsey's *Discover Australia's Golf Courses* was the authoritative directory of where we could find the country's finest golf.

In early 2001, I had the good fortune of playing a Greg Norman-designed course in the company of our foremost golf writer, Tom Ramsey, with discussions invariably leading to Australia's best new courses and how they compared to the classics. During the conversation I was struck by just how far the industry had come in the years since Ramsey's famous publication and how much the landscape has changed since the Alister MacKenzie-inspired golden age of Australian golf in the 1920s and 1930s.

This golden age left the country with not only a series of outstanding courses but also the inspiration for subsequent generations of golf course architects. However, following the Great Depression right through to the mid-1980s, there was plenty of design activity but strangely few courses of any real quality. In fact, the most significant work during this period consisted of redesigns at The Lakes and The Australian, and the relocated Royal Canberra Course at Westbourne Woods.

Despite a decrease in the quantity of new course production, this 'Modern' (post-1985) era has, in my view, become the first prolonged period of quality golf architecture seen in Australia since MacKenzie left our shores. Chapter 1, 'From MacKenzie to Moonah', outlines the outstanding courses of both eras and analyses whether the perennial reign of courses such as Royal Melbourne, Kingston Heath and New South Wales atop ranking lists is finally under threat. It also looks at some of the recent design trends, both positive and negative, and the effect of the modern game on classic courses trying to keep pace.

The most obvious trend in modern course design is increased length as we seemingly push on towards the 7000-metre golf course. Easily blamed on the technology of golf equipment, the real issue is the marketability of 'championship length' golf and the ego of designers determined to defend their par. While traditionally all players enjoyed golf from the same tees, the stretched course has taken this equilibrium away and placed an absolute, and in my opinion unhealthy, reliance on multiple teeing options. In order to provide fair and balanced reviews, each course featured, modern or classic, was seen from the championship tees with any reference to distance, carry, shape or driving lines taken from the very back markers.

Throughout the book conditioning is afforded only scant consideration and often overlooked, despite considerable improvement in the overall standard of course presentation. It is always unfair to judge a course by its turf as many are only seen once or twice and not always at their best. Describing turf quality can also distort reality and I would hate to turn golfers off a wonderfully raw course like Newcastle because its perfectly playable fairways did not offer the same striped lines of lush lies available at nearby resorts.

Naturally there are exceptions, most notably the ultra-exclusive Capital and Ellerston courses, where grooming excellence is part of the experience. Lloyd Williams' Capital is better known and also more popular, with as many as ten patrons taking divots on a typical day compared with an average of one round every two days at Kerry Packer's Ellerston Golf Course. With a full complement of greenkeepers, it is little wonder they are kept in such phenomenal condition, but believe me both exceed even your wildest golfing fantasies. As neither course is accessible to the golfing public I am particularly pleased to be able to take readers behind the security gates to provide a sample of these courses' incredible hidden beauty.

Although my personal preferences become apparent in the Ratings chapter, I should preface the book by explaining that the courses featured were seen through the eyes of a passionate golfer who believes there is no such thing as a bad day on the links. It is written as a tribute to the country's top courses and with more than 1600 to choose from, any track that has made the final selection is worthy of celebration whether it be good, great or out of this world.

With superb photography and leading course designers providing anecdotes and design philosophies on most of the modern tracks, my hope is that you will find this an insightful read and an indispensable guide to the best of Australian golf.

Packer's playground, the incredible Ellerston Golf Course. Picture taken from beside the 13th green.

FROM MACKENZIE TO MOONAH

F licking through these pages or reviewing any list that ranks Australian golf courses, it is clear that this country has experienced two periods of high quality golf design— the classic years of the 1920s to 30s, and the present, post-1985, modern era.

From MacKenzie ...

The pre-Depression era is recognised throughout the world as the golden age of golf course architecture, famous for the work of design luminaries such as Colt, Ross, Flynn and Tillinghast. In Australia, however, there is just one name synonymous with this period: Dr Alister MacKenzie. The legendary British designer visited our shores towards the end of 1926, and, though his trip lasted a few short weeks, his legacy will live forever.

When MacKenzie arrived in Australia the game of golf was booming. Melbourne's Sandbelt had been discovered and was flourishing, and clubs throughout the country were increasing in popularity. Almost without exception, however, the Australian golf course was over-bunkered, penal and set up with narrow fairways and cramped playing areas. MacKenzie immediately identified these architectural deficiencies and, believing his philosophies would not only improve the courses but also the standard of play, managed to convince an entire industry that, with reform, it was potentially world-class.

Having previously penned his famous Thirteen Rules of Great Golf Design, MacKenzie brought to Australia one commandment in particular that would define his influence on the game here: 'There should be a sufficient number of heroic carries from the tee, but the course should be arranged so that the weaker player, with the loss of a stroke, has an alternate route to the green'. By shifting the design mindset from penal to strategic he gave the average Australian golfer options and the scratch player the inspiration to improve.

MacKenzie was indeed fortunate to have great land at his disposal. He was even more fortunate to find a greenkeeper like Mick Morcom who not only understood his principles but also had the skill to construct his incredible shapes. Evidence of Morcom's tremendous talent can be seen in the exquisite contouring of greens and bunkers scattered throughout the Melbourne Sandbelt, which are mostly his work and still as astonishing as ever.

Another factor that should not be forgotten is MacKenzie's dictum that par was an abstract concept and his belief that a golfer's focus should instead be on enjoying a full round in 'even fours'. Many of his 2-shot holes were actually designed as 2½-shot holes with attractive 'introducing' bunkers set some way short of the greens, and built not to impede the average player but instead tempt the better players trying to shave a stroke.

Whether they be single traps or a series of bunkers diagonally invading the target line, today these magnificent hazards retain an enormous visual value despite at times offering little strategic difficulty for the modern golfer. The combination of their beauty and the timelessness of the intrinsic strategy have ensured that the MacKenzie courses, and those he inspired, remain eternally popular.

Previous spread: Royal Melbourne, West Course 2nd hole.

Opposite page: MacKenzie's magnificent par three 5th hole at Royal Melbourne West.

... to Moonah

This modern era is more difficult to categorise and for the sake of a definition alone is described as post-1985. The Australian golfscape began changing in the mid-1980s with the introduction of many of today's prolific designers and the advent of American-style resort golf. Consistent with trends throughout the world, we also saw the arrival of 'signature design' with the marketability of high-profile names such as Greg Norman, Jack Nicklaus and Peter Thomson used to generate interest and secure financial backing for new course development.

Following an initial boom we have slowly seen a shift away from the American style of design towards a natural, more traditional Australian style with the notion of wall-to-wall turf replaced by the use of native grasses and the concept of 'finishing' the look of a course. While the majority of new course development remains on reclaimed or degraded land, the success of traditional design has encouraged the search for traditional land with a bevy of spectacular golf sites consequently unearthed, complemented by some outstanding layouts.

Despite the undeniable quality of many newcomers and the worldwide trend toward building a longer golf course, the time-honoured classics remain entrenched atop our popular ranking lists. Whether this is entirely based on the quality of the product or a reluctance to diminish the status of established courses is debatable, but what is clear is that the trend in golf course length has shifted forever.

Back in 1926 MacKenzie believed the designer's primary obligation was to provide the membership with what he described as 'pleasurable enjoyment'. Despite a lasting reverence to 'short' courses like Royal Melbourne, it seems today's designers are instead driven by the concept of 'championship length'.

The modern tracks featured in this book are, on average, more than 200 metres longer than the classics; the Open Course at Moonah Links is a staggering 400 metres further again. *Golf Digest*'s recent ranking list also supports the evidence of this trend, with just a handful of courses in Australia's Top 50 shorter than either course at Royal Melbourne, and each was built prior to 1950. This is in spite of the acknowledged challenge our classic courses still present the world's best players and more than 70 years of rankings domination.

Aside from being longer, today's courses are also more difficult, with course ratings now regularly reaching up to five strokes above par, which was unheard of until the likes of Sanctuary Cove Pines came along. It appears that while MacKenzie dismissed the notion of par, the modern designer has reinstated it and chosen to defend it to the death against players better equipped to defeat it than ever before. The unfortunate victim of longer, tougher golf is the average player who is still hampered by bad technique, and for whom the game throughout Australia, and the world, is getting harder. For these golfers, forward tees and titanium are not just an option but a necessity.

And so from the weeks that revolutionised golf in this country through to an era where a 6800-metre monster was custom built to host the National Open, the game of golf in Australia has certainly come a long way from MacKenzie to Moonah.

Opposite page: The attractive (and relatively simple) opening hole on Australia's longest golf course, the Open Course at Moonah Links.

The Classic Classic
versus the Modern Masterpiece

In order to introduce you to Australia's best golf we begin by showcasing the finest examples of golf course architecture within the Classic and Modern eras. Interestingly each featured classic is a MacKenzie course, to varying degrees, while the contemporary courses are all, in some part, shaped by local British Open champions. By selecting just four in each category, many wonderful courses have been left out, but all eight selected are clear standouts.

The chosen classics are all world-class and range from the full MacKenzie design at Royal Melbourne West through to Royal Adelaide where only the odd remnant of his work remains.

Royal Melbourne was the club that brought MacKenzie to Australia and he did not disappoint, leaving them the archetypal Australian golf course and the standard by which every subsequent course is judged. Acting as consultant he then moved to Kingston Heath where he recognised the quality of the existing layout and complemented it by planning, arguably, the most intricate and awesome bunkering system ever seen. He also added a touch of poetry at the short 15th, which if not the best par three in Australia, is certainly on the short-list. Admittedly Dan Soutar worked wonders on the small property and his routing is rightfully acclaimed.

Travelling to La Perouse in Sydney, MacKenzie then designed the New South Wales golf course on what he conceded was a difficult site to finish. The bunkering was left until the club could establish patterns of play, with local architect Eric Apperly entrusted to finish the job. Although Apperly also changed the course significantly from its first routing, it remains MacKenzie who chose to set holes dramatically up and over the awesome ridges and hills instead of through the valleys, which maximised the thrills of a spectacular site.

MacKenzie left Australia to design Cypress Point and Augusta National in the United States, but on his way out stopped off in Adelaide where Royal Adelaide presented him with one of the great sites in world golf. Unlike Kingston Heath, he identified distinct flaws with the set-up he saw and mapped a detailed alternative. Strangely his mere presence seemed to divide the club, and although they did not embrace his ideas entirely, they did build his mind-boggling short 3rd hole and over time added a number of others, including the brilliant 14th. The modern Royal Adelaide is more penal than the other three but retains the ageless and unconventional charm that it developed during this period.

Despite strong claims to the contrary, the view that MacKenzie was the equal if not overriding influence on each of these courses is a belief I share. This may seem unjust to men like Soutar and Apperly considering MacKenzie only did the bunkering at Kingston Heath and part of the routing at New South Wales but despite the differences, for me, both courses are world-class because of the MacKenzie touches.

Although touched by the same man, these four courses are remarkably diverse, as are the four featured from this modern era. Capital is an incredible concept with the course custom-built by millionaire businessman Lloyd Williams for the exclusive enjoyment of those around him. More money was spent shaping the holes and surroundings here than on any course in Australia, as every square metre of its 300-acre site was totally transformed from flat market gardens into a pure golfing oasis.

In direct contrast, the National Moonah and Kennedy Bay courses are about as natural as the game gets with the golf holes 'discovered' rather than created. Construction costs were less than a tenth of those at Capital yet both are sophisticated, thrilling and tremendously original with Kennedy Bay one of the most genuine links-like experiences outside of Britain, and Moonah one of the most spectacular.

The final featured modern course is Ellerston, an extraordinary private playground built for the Packer family and set high in the New South Wales Upper Hunter Valley. The very fact the course is highlighted as Australia's premier modern track demands comparison to the MacKenzie masterpiece at Royal Melbourne. In truth they could not be more dissimilar; nor, however, is their appeal more apparent.

Ellerston designers Norman and Harrison had no obligation to the average golfer and met their client's brief to create Australia's toughest course by building a series of exhilarating holes that most would find totally unplayable. Playability is, of course, the very quality that sets Royal Melbourne apart; in direct contrast to Norman and Harrison, MacKenzie was handed a list of ages and handicaps prior to design to ensure his West Course was 'fair' to all members. For 95 per cent of golfers, therefore, Royal Melbourne remains the pinnacle. But for those capable of hitting the shots and who have the opportunity to do so Ellerston is unforgettable and few places on earth can rival it.

While Ellerston is a 'once in a lifetime' experience, Royal Melbourne remains a 'course for the ages', and with breathtaking settings and brilliant design the question of superiority has become a matter of 'pleasurable enjoyment' for all versus the 'ultimate challenge' for a select few.

The inspiring 17th at Royal Melbourne West, showing off MacKenzie's genius design and Morcom's sublime sculpting.

Classic Classics

The Royal Melbourne Golf Club, West Course

Course opened: 1931
Designer: Dr Alister MacKenzie

The dangerous but drivable 10th at Royal Melbourne West, one of Australian golf's great short par fours.

That Royal Melbourne is Australia's foremost golf club is irrefutable. For more than 100 years the club has been at the pinnacle of the game in this country, its golf courses the most celebrated in the Southern Hemisphere. Volumes have been written on the qualities of the West Course; put simply, it's a combination of the greatest land, greatest design and greatest construction ever seen in this country that makes it so special. As local designer Michael Clayton says, 'it is one of only two man-made things in Australia of worldwide significance'.

It all began in 1891 when a group of prominent Melburnians formally introduced 'the Royal and Ancient game' to Victoria by establishing the Melbourne Golf Club on leased land near the Caulfield railway station. As urban encroachment threatened the existence of their course, the search for a more permanent home brought the club's council to a racetrack built among the heathland scrub of Sandringham in the city's south. What they uncovered among the undulating sand dunes was the ideal location for their new links, a discovery that inadvertently led to the birth of the Melbourne Sandbelt.

The club's Sandringham course opened for play in 1901, but by the early 1920s housing had engulfed the western corner of the course. The club decided to sell this part of the site and move slightly east to their main paddock in Black Rock where an additional 68 acres of land were available. Although only six of the original holes were lost in the relocation, it was decided that the entire course should be upgraded and redesigned.

A committee that included Australian Open champion Alex Russell was given authority to seek the best golf course architect available to advise on the new layout, and to do so regardless of cost. At the time the Royal and Ancient Golf Club at St Andrews was using Dr Alister MacKenzie as a consultant, and recommended him to the club's President who was in Britain at the time. For a fee of £1000, MacKenzie accepted the invitation to advise at Royal Melbourne, and in 1926 started his groundbreaking Australasian adventure. Though this fee was steep, the club recovered most of its expenses by acting as the designer's agent, collecting a share of the monies he collected from a further eighteen clubs that used his services.

His stay in Black Rock was brief. While on-site to survey the land he was accompanied by Russell and head greenkeeper Mick Morcom who was well read on the subject of golf architecture. MacKenzie was clearly satisfied that both men were capable of interpreting his ideas and philosophies and when he departed he left the construction of his West Course to their supervision. He later described Morcom as the best greenkeeper he had ever come across and appointed Russell as his design partner.

The site remains one of the finest ever found in world golf. Full of dramatic undulation, its fertile sandy soil and natural rugged appearance were gifts from the golfing gods. Before starting work on the design, MacKenzie asked for a listing of all member's ages and handicaps, determined to make his course enjoyable for golfers of any ability. The timeless strategy of his subsequent design is as profound as it is simplistic; it is based around wide fairways that are playable to the average golfer yet demand the best players drive the ball into the corners to get close to the flags. When the greens are at their fearsome best this is not an easy thing to do.

Picking out West Course highlights is as difficult as mounting a compelling argument against its long-held position atop Australian golf rankings. Visually, Morcom's bold bunkering is spectacular while the rough areas around the tees and bunkers are a mix of native grasses which beautifully and naturally frame each hole, providing great definition and contrast without distracting from the strategy.

The greens are simply brilliant and for decades have consistently provided the finest putting surfaces in Australia. Large and beautifully contoured, they are built to accommodate approaches from a number of angles with each progressively more difficult the further the tee shot strays from the perfect line.

Individually there are at least ten outstanding holes, including six that are undeniably world-class like the all-carry par three 5th with its awesome bunkering and slippery raised green pressed against a magnificent scrub-covered dune. When MacKenzie first saw this inspired setting he enthusiastically declared that they should be able to make

one of the best golf holes in existence. Morcom didn't let the genius designer down, building an exquisite hole, which was, in fact, the only one he constructed under MacKenzie's direct supervision.

The 6th hole is also remarkable and has become a textbook par four, highlighting all that is challenging and fair about the designer's commandments of golf architecture. Its grand sweeping fairway, tantalising corner bunkers and superb green setting are as playable to the first-timer as they are thrilling to the professional. For many, this is golf's best par four.

There are plenty of other standouts including the driveable 10th hole, with its teasing target perched beyond the largest and deepest sand hazard in the country, and the breathtaking greenside bunkering at the 17th. The final hole is also famous with a thrilling tee shot played across a steep sandy ridge to a blind dipping fairway.

Both tee and green on the 18th have been shifted since MacKenzie departed but, like the majority of alterations made through the years, the changes have been minor. The obvious exception is the 7th hole, built by Ivo Whitton in the late 1930s to allow extra room for the first tee on the East Course. The green on the 12th was also shifted significantly to the left and slightly back to create a wonderful kink at the end of the fairway.

Perhaps the most interesting change was that made to the 15th long after MacKenzie had discovered the penal artificial mounding of the existing hole and declared 'we'll leave it as is, to show future generations how silly golf course architecture used to be'. The fact he left this deliberate blemish to underline the inadequacies of penal design shows he was probably a man who did not believe in the notion of the perfect golf course. Although his point was well made, years later the club improved the hole by removing the central section of these mounds.

It seems a great shame that MacKenzie never saw the finished product at Royal Melbourne because, despite leaving our shores to create countless classics across the globe, there is little doubt the West Course retains the purest interpretation of his design philosophies.

Gene Sarazen said it best many years ago when he famously quipped, 'it burns me up that with the billions of dollars spent on course construction in the past fifty years, all the architects together haven't been able to build another Royal Melbourne'.

It is certainly hard to imagine that the game of golf gets any better than Royal Melbourne West. From purist to mug punter and professional, it remains the embodiment of golfing perfection, if indeed such a thing exists.

Kingston Heath Golf Club

Course opened: 1925
Designers: Dan Soutar, Dr Alister MacKenzie

Shortly after World War I, prominent Melbourne solicitor Stanley Dutton Green led a committee of members from the Elsternwick Golf Club in a search to acquire land within the Melbourne Sandbelt to construct their own championship golf course. The search for the ideal site took them south to Cheltenham and a small gently undulating parcel of land with a perfect sandy soil and a number of excellent natural features.

Fascinated by British design, Green had corresponded with two of golf's biggest names, Open champions J.H. Taylor and Harry Vardon, who convinced him that, with the advent of the rubber-cored ball, the new course should be built of a length to 'stand the test of time'. The committee agreed and called in Sydney professional Dan Soutar to design the layout.

Soutar walked the property twice without comment before coming to rest amidst dense scrub near the centre of the site and declaring 'here is where we start, an ideal ready-made short hole for the 10th'. He later famously changed the direction of the 10th hole, but continued to plan the entire course from this point.

When the course was ready for play in 1925, it had met the club's brief and was officially the longest ever seen in Australia. Measuring a little over 6200 metres, its bogey (par) of 82 included twelve par fives and just two par threes. Golfers who today lament trends toward the 7000-metre course should be thankful they were not around to tackle 'the Heath' in its infancy armed with a hickory shafted Brassie and Niblick.

The short par four 9th shows off the Heath's unique mix of hazards and heathlands. The MacKenzie bunkering transformed what was brutal into something beautiful.

Royal Melbourne had kindly offered the services of its head greenkeeper Mick Morcom to assist with the building of fairways, tees and greens while the bunkering was deferred on news of the imminent arrival of famed architect Dr Alister MacKenzie. In town to design Royal Melbourne West, MacKenzie also advised on the bunkering at several courses within the Sandbelt, leaving his most significant mark on Kingston Heath.

After one inspection of the site he enthused that 'never yet have I advised upon a course where, owing to the excellence of design and construction work, the problems have been so simple'. Despite some reservations about its length, he clearly thought highly of Soutar's routing, while the construction had impressed him to the point of proclaiming Morcom the best he had ever encountered at his craft.

Aside from providing detailed reports on the bunkering of each hole MacKenzie also felt compelled to suggest one important change to the overall course design, converting the blind par four 15th hole into an ingenious uphill par three. Often criticised for being obstinate, the fact he could find just one design fault was in itself a glowing endorsement of the Soutar layout.

It is interesting to note that the designer was paid £25 for his tireless work while the club reluctantly paid MacKenzie ten times that amount for bunkering plans that he finished in a matter of days. Though seemingly inequitable, the club was left with one of the country's truly great par threes, and possibly the best bunkering system in the world. Today it must feel like the best £250 they ever spent.

With the exception of dense tea-tree and heavy undergrowth that was badly burnt out following a major wildfire in 1944, the natural process of the course's evolution has gone relatively smoothly. Recent years have seen the club look to combat problems associated with

From a blind par four to an incredible par three, MacKenzie's remarkable 15th.

The 10th at Kingston Heath,
'an ideal ready-made short hole'.

overplanting by removing a series of old mahogany gums and cypresses, focusing instead on restoring the vast areas of low growing heath grasses that give the course its unique character. The balance between the stands of trees and open areas of native grasses is important to Kingston Heath, as part of its charm is the manner in which the holes and hazards seamlessly integrate into the surrounding vegetation.

Most of the modern course alterations were made by long-time superintendent Graeme Grant, including the rebuilding of several greens, and the successful addition of a deep depression protecting the front of the reachable par five 7th. There was also the controversial placement of a new bunker in the centre of the 11th fairway prior to an Australian Open, which has been less well received. The putting surfaces, especially those Grant reshaped during his tenure, are superb, and it would be hard to argue that the greens on any classic course in Australia, other than perhaps Royal Melbourne, are better than the Heath's.

The course also boasts an astonishing collection of par threes, the signature 15th coupled with beautifully shaped and bunkered short holes at the 5th and 10th. Of the remaining holes, aside from a number of fascinating blind and semi-blind shots, the highlight is the driveable but deadly par four 3rd. Contoured to reward only the most precise pitch shot, this outstanding green is angled across the fairway and surrounded by exquisite bunkering.

Though Kingston Heath no longer plays like the monster it once was, the combination of an ageless design and stupendous bunkering has made holes like 3, 9, 10 and 15 technology-proof and helped the course stand the ultimate test of time. Its greatest defence against low scoring remains a strategic layout that is playable to all yet demands absolute precision from the professional wanting to score birdies.

Enjoying a reputation as one of the world's finest tracks, Kingston Heath remains a supreme test of golfing smarts. The course is a special privilege to play and one of the finest examples of golf course architecture from any era.

New South Wales Golf Club

Course opened: 1928
Designers: Dr Alister MacKenzie, Eric Apperly

While the architecture at Royal Melbourne and Kingston Heath may be more sophisticated, few courses of any era are as compelling and spectacular as the timeless classic at the New South Wales Golf Club.

Situated on the rugged cliffs at La Perouse, the New South Wales Golf Club overlooks Botany Bay where Captain James Cook first sailed into Australia aboard the Endeavour in 1770. For golfers, however, it was the visit of another intrepid British pioneer which gives the site its historical significance.

During his whirlwind 1926 Australian tour, Dr Alister MacKenzie visited La Perouse and enthused about the potential for building a great golf course. Clearly moved by the surroundings, he declared that New South Wales would 'present more spectacular views than any other golf course in the world, with the possible exception of Cypress Point'. Today golfers continue to make the pilgrimage to this sacred site to tackle a course built by nature, framed by the Pacific Ocean and shaped by the greatest hand of all.

The success of the golf course cannot be solely credited to the genius of MacKenzie, as the work of Eric Apperly in completing the architect's plans after he departed was also

The view from behind Apperly's outstanding ocean carry par three 6th.

*The 15th hole at New South Wales
Golf Club from behind the green.*

outstanding. While MacKenzie mapped the routing, the bunkers were left to Apperly, who also made a number of changes to the layout during the subsequent years. Most significant was the building of the world-renowned 6th hole in the 1930s, and the shifting of the 5th tee after the army reclaimed land during World War II. These two holes are individually among Australia's best; collectively they are one of the most awe-inspiring double acts in world golf.

The tee on 5 was originally positioned on an elevated sand dune left of its current location with the rugged Cape Banks shoreline visible from the tee. After the war it was moved inland, near MacKenzie's original 4th tee, making the hole straighter and the tee shot blind over an enormous rise. With a breeze at your back the hill can be cleared and the green often reached with little more than a driver then a wedge, while into a headwind it can take up to three woods to get home. From the summit of the fairway the hole plunges dramatically almost 30 metres down towards a tiny target and the mighty Pacific Ocean. The vista here of falling fairway and crashing waves is quite simply the most magnificent in Australian golf.

Equally memorable is the fabulous par three 6th, played from a rocky outcrop behind the 5th green over the sea to a small sloping green back on the mainland. Interestingly, this was not originally part of MacKenzie's plan, the oversight possibly due to the land not being available for use when he first saw the site. Considering he left Australia to finish work on Cypress Point, which boasts the most famous Ocean carry par three in the world, it seems doubtful that when looking to thrill he would have missed the opportunity for such an obvious showstopper. Completing a stunning loop along the coast, the uphill 7th is another wonderful hole and one of the few untouched MacKenzie originals.

A second coastal loop on the back nine, 13 through 16, is also world-class with a series of difficult par fours played along and away from the cliffs. The stunning short 14th is a smiling assassin featuring extreme fairway contouring that is so naturally spectacular the ocean outlook appears almost insignificant. Offering no respite, the 15th is the hardest hole on the course and demands a strong, straight tee shot through a narrow chute of dunes and tea-tree to reach a saddle at the fairway's crest. Missing the drive usually means reloading, while a good tee shot here sets up an uninterrupted view of a beautiful green site shifted almost 100 metres to its present position by Apperly during the 1930s.

Magnificently wild and exposed, the entire course offers tremendous views and a series of stunning holes built around, over and through the hills and valleys that lead towards the coastline. The routing, as much as the setting, makes New South Wales special, and despite more than 70 years of change and evolution, twelve holes and the majority of the standout moments remain either Mackenzie originals or variations on a theme he first suggested. Of those altered the most noticeable are the four Apperly par threes, which form the best set of short holes in Sydney, and the par five 8th which is a combination of MacKenzie's 7th and 8th.

Given the great man's enormous reputation for designing bunkers, the decision to entrust Apperly with the building of his signature hazards, once patterns of play had been established, was also an exceptional stroke of humility from an otherwise voracious character. The bunkering, though not as brilliant as Kingston Heath and Royal Melbourne, is nonetheless strategic and well-suited to the landscape. A recently completed restoration program involved rebuilding the more exposed traps with a traditional revetted face and was very successful.

The other significant improvement made to the course in modern times came when, in 1998, wildfires tore through the site destroying trees and seriously threatening the course and clubhouse. Though stressful at the time, the clearing of shrubs along the course's periphery has actually improved the views and enhanced the experience.

Shortly after its 1928 opening, an edition of the *Golf in Australia* magazine described New South Wales as needing 'only the improving hand of time to become the acme of perfection'. The hand of time has indeed improved this masterpiece, and though it is unlikely that any course is the absolute 'acme of perfection', New South Wales Golf Club gets about as close as any in Australia.

Falling fairway and crashing waves—the view from the right rough on the stunning par five 5th hole.

Royal Adelaide Golf Club

Course opened: 1905
Designers: H.L. Rymill, C.L. Gardiner, Dr Alister MacKenzie

Despite the tremendous quality of the courses featured in this book, for me no track in Australia is as interesting as Royal Adelaide. Without the construction brilliance of a Royal Melbourne or the exhilaration of a New South Wales, the course simply wins you over with its unique design and distinctive charm.

Founded as the Adelaide Golf Club at Glenelg in 1892, the club moved to its present Seaton site in 1904. Ideal for golf with wild sandy craters and towering dunes, the land also housed a municipal train station (now the pro shop) which provided members with easy access to their links.

The first course was a modest design by committee members C.L. Gardiner and H.L. Rymill and opened for play in 1905. Rymill, who later founded Kooyonga, then upgraded the course in 1908, adding a thousand yards and incorporating the sand hills into the routing as well as several railway crossings. A subsequent beautification program introduced the magnificent pines to the site and transformed the raw coastal sandscape into a grand scale golfing experience.

Like so many of our best classics, the course received its most notable overhaul when Dr Alister MacKenzie made a flying visit to Adelaide in 1926 after designing Royal Melbourne West. Mightily impressed with the terrain, he was particularly excited by the abundance of sand, proclaiming that 'no seaside courses that I have seen possess such magnificent sand craters as those at Royal Adelaide'.

Though only in town for a few short days he worked fast, preparing a report which reconfigured the 18 holes to eliminate dangerous rail crossings, and recommended converting many of the penal fairway bunkers into undulating ground. He also insisted on making full use of the site's natural features by designing holes over and around the enormous dunes. He departed the club, boasting that 'if the suggestions put forward for the

The 14th, one of the many strong par fours at Royal Adelaide.

reconstruction of the Royal Adelaide course are acted upon, it will be superior to most, if not all, English championship courses'.

His proposal, however, was not universally accepted and, immediately following his departure, heavy debate within the club led to a number of ideas being renounced. Despite his persuasive character and lofty reputation, the members refused to be totally beholden to the plans of a brash foreigner and instead chose to initially pick out the best bits of his designs and ignore the rest.

They built his inspired short par four 3rd hole, which hasn't changed, and the awesome sand crater drive at the dogleg 4th, which remains a MacKenzie moment despite the hole being stretched almost 100 metres beyond what he had intended. Eleven greens were also rebuilt and over time the 6th, 9th, 13th and 14th were altered to resemble MacKenzie's original plan.

The 13th tee was only moved to its current position in the 1990s when, in preparation for the 1998 Australian Open, the course underwent its most notable and controversial upgrade since the 1920s. Under the guidance of Peter Thomson and Michael Wolveridge, the fairways were narrowed, rough thickened, and a number of strong back tees built. The cramped driving areas on these extended holes are particularly penal on the mid-marker and a further departure from the MacKenzie ideal of generous, strategic fairways that are playable to all golfers. The pair did add a beautifully understated lateral hazard left of the green on the quirky closing 'road' hole, which has been a revelation.

These modifications were considered necessary by the event's tournament committee and probably viewed as a success in light of the fact none of the professionals was able to break par. In truth, though, the changes have done little to improve the golf course and those brought about by the MacKenzie visit remain the most significant seen at Seaton. Aside from helping members realise the potential of their amazing site, his gift to the club was to leave behind the most extraordinary short par four this part of the world has ever seen.

By my reckoning there are almost 25,000 golf holes in Australia and, for me, the sole MacKenzie hole remaining at Royal Adelaide, the 3rd, may be the best of the lot. Though a

An Australian classic—the 3rd hole at Royal Adelaide from behind the green.

visionary, he had no way of foreseeing the technological advances in our modern game yet managed to build a short blind par four along an enormous dune that remains as mesmerising when played with titanium as it was with hickory.

The genius of his design is in the positioning of the green beneath the towering dune, and the scruffy knoll and small ridge that guard its narrow front. From the tee, the critical decision is which club to take and whether to play safely to the top of the crest or head over the hill towards the green. The penalties are greater the more aggressive you get but the approach more difficult the safer you play. An accurate tee shot with the driver equals a probable birdie and the straight lay-up a comfortable par, yet stray with either shot and you are left fighting for a five.

The other 'obvious' standout at Royal Adelaide is number 11, the infamous 'Crater Hole'. With the tee shifted back against the boundary fence, the hole is now a mid-length par four played towards the peak of a rising fairway then over a huge sandy crater to a green framed by an imposing pine-covered sand hill. Pushing the green site right back into the dune was actually MacKenzie's idea, although his plan for a dogleg from near the present 10th tee was rejected.

Holes like the 3rd and 11th became legends in this country long ago and are duly preserved, while the continued tweaking of others like 4, 8, 13, 14 and 18 has seen them also elevated to a similar status.

Royal Adelaide is one of a kind and unquestionably the most unusual and offbeat classic course in the country. A triumph of commonsense management, the course has changed substantially over the years, yet retained its fundamental character and charm. No two holes are the same and, better still, no two are even remotely alike. Sure there are flaws but there are also brilliant moments that almost defy description.

The greatest golf courses break the mould and successfully challenge the accepted principles and practices of popular golf design. Royal Adelaide is clearly such a course, and though it may not be golf's most perfect, to many it is golf's most enjoyable.

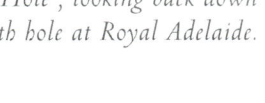

'Crater Hole', looking back down the 11th hole at Royal Adelaide.

Modern Masterpieces

Ellerston Golf Course

Course opened: 2001
Designers: Greg Norman, Bob Harrison

'Golf's new benchmark.'

Locked away in the secluded high country of the New South Wales Upper Hunter lies Ellerston, a veritable Shangri-la preserved for the exclusive enjoyment of Australia's wealthiest family. For lovers of the equine pursuits, this remarkable property has long been a landmark, for within its natural valleys and tumbling hills are pristine polo fields recognised as the finest throughout the world. The property has now set a new benchmark—this time for golf.

Despite its inaccessibility to the golfing public, cataloguing the country's finest golf courses without including the Packer family's private facility would leave the directory incomplete. Simply put, this is the most extraordinary golf course built in Australia since the Great Depression.

Attractive and expensive, Ellerston's par three 6th hole.

The inspiration behind media tycoon Kerry Packer's decision to build his Ellerston course is unclear, but when he propositioned Greg Norman Golf Design in 1999, his objective was unambiguous. The firm was to build him Australia's toughest and most spectacular golf course.

With budget unlikely to be a problem the critical issue became selecting the best site. Initially cliffs overlooking Byron Bay were considered, but when they proved inadequate, the design team was given carte blanche to select any site within Packer's 70,000 acre sanctuary.

'For me Ellerston was a very special project. It had taken me more than ten years to convince my good friend and passionate golfer, Kerry Packer, that he should build his own golf course, and when the decision was finally made he ensured the brief was unique. Create the best golf course possible with as few tees as possible; in other words, build a golf course that penalises poor shots, makes the golfer think and play hard. He got all that plus more.

'The land at our disposal was ideal, and the natural features as well as the flora and fauna were so spectacular that very few routings were actually done as the holes virtually mapped themselves. We had no need to consider forward tees, resort traffic or weaker hitters, and could make the carries demanding and the holes as formidable as required. The whole process proved particularly enjoyable, as we were able to create a course that a golfer of my calibre would love to play everyday for the rest of his life.

Following several days scouring the vast area, the fast-flowing and beautiful Pages Creek was discovered and instantly recognised as the perfect location around which to build the dramatic course Packer desired. The creek is the central feature of the layout and incorporated into no fewer than nine holes, including five where it dramatically cuts directly in front of greens. Wary of its overuse, however, the design was balanced by building almost half the course in higher country leading away from the hazard. Rather than suffering by comparison, these elevated holes are every bit as breathtaking and provide some of the round's most memorable moments.

Fanatical about the difficulty level of the course, the client's determination to provide the ultimate challenge to the world's best players was unyielding. This attitude enabled the designers to take more risks than usual, creating shots and sequences that simply would not be possible on a publically accessible course, and building a number of spectacular green sites hard against the edge of the rapidly running creek. One such site, the 6th, was actually washed away by heavy rains shortly after the course opened. This had not been entirely unexpected given the areas propensity to flood; to alleviate the worry and expense of continually rebuilding the green, an elevated alternative was suggested. Without hesitation however Packer ordered the green be rebuilt exactly where it was and to do so each time it washed away.

Without a single indifferent moment, the highlights at Ellerston come thick and fast, especially through the front nine holes, which contain the bulk of the awe-inspiring scenes and as many as eight holes considered for the Ratings chapter at the end of this book.

The opening tee shot sets the tone for the round with a glorious set of bunkers built into a gentle rise that not only defines the driving line of the first fairway but also the journey you are about to embark on. Falling away as it nears the green, this fascinating par five introduces golfers to the lowland features of the site. Holes then continue on this lower ground, alongside the creek, before heading into the high country from the 8th and not returning until a rousing downhill plunge on the par three 15th.

The long and demanding par fours are particularly impressive, and are relentless on your driving with each requiring a long bomb positioned in the premium part of the fairway to ensure

an unimpeded line into the treacherous greens. Eight of these measure between 430 and 460 yards, yet as a set they are remarkably diverse thanks to constant elevation change and the sometimes subtle, sometimes salient use of contrasting hazards. The 7th and 8th are wonderful illustrations with the downhill 7th measuring 45 metres longer than the 8th but generally playing at least a club shorter. The tee shot at the 7th is truly incredible, with an elevated tee built into the side of a hill that forces the drive to be played down the length of a river towards the fairway some 200 yards away. The intimidating 8th hole then heads back up the hill with its approach crossing a cavernous gully towards a green perched virtually out on a ledge.

Equally thrilling are the back-to-back par fives at 9 and 10, both with incredibly attractive green sites and fairways that demand strong and precise tee shots. The 9th is a risk/reward drive across a series of diagonal bunkers followed by a steep downhill plunge through a narrow forest, while the 10th requires a full throttle uphill drive that needs to work off a large gum in the fairway. A gully then runs up the length of the hole with the pitch across the hazard to a beautifully contoured green being one of the course highlights.

With relative respite offered through the 15th, the excitement returns in spades at the audacious 16th, a totally unique concept I suspect the designers had never previously dared consider. The approach here is an awesome all-or-nothing carry up the length of the creek, towards a spectacular target framed by a sheer cliff face and encircled by the creek's running water. Spray the shot and you will need to reload, but pull it off, as I did with my four iron, and it's just about the most exhilarating feeling in golf.

Throughout the round the variety and beauty of the green settings, whether dramatically pushed hard up against the creek or set in natural gullies or atop small ridges, is quite striking. Most are framed visually by the impressive Norman/Harrison bunker shapes, although bunkerless targets like the 5th, 10th and 16th are among Ellerston's most attractive. The actual putting surfaces are immense and without equal, rolling as fast and true as Royal Melbourne's in their prime yet without a single blemish. Designed for great speeds, the contouring can be quite subtle and generally follows the movement of the surrounding landscape.

Previous page: Not for the faint-hearted, the thrilling drive down the 7th fairway.

This page: One of golf's most daring holes, Ellerston's astonishing 16th.

'Even more pleasing was being able to tour the property shortly after construction with a delighted owner as he surveyed his finished course for the first time. From the outset, we knew the potential was enormous, but I am nevertheless ecstatic with the result, as Ellerston is clearly one of the best golf courses in Australia.'
Greg Norman

The beautifully contoured 10th green, set into a small hill across a gully.

The presentation of the golf course is impossible to fault and it would be foolish to try—analysis of even the worst turf here makes every other course in Australia seem substandard. Pure Santa Ana Couch is used in the fairways and Pennlinks Bentgrass on the greens, while the short roughs comprise a Buffalo mix to provide a contrasting colour and texture. This Buffalo grass does not wear particularly well and is unsuitable for courses with even moderate traffic levels; it is fortunate, therefore, that Ellerston averages just three rounds per week!

Although I am a strong advocate of quality design over quality grooming, a pampering at Ellerston opens your eyes to what can actually be achieved on a golfing field. Prior to my visit there had not been a single round in six days, and with the fairways double cut, what I experienced was pure golfing opulence.

In terms of site, design, conditioning, challenge and exhilaration, the bar has been raised impossibly high, with the quality of each modern course in this book, regardless of the superlatives used in its review, relative to Ellerston. Like Royal Melbourne West to the classics, the contemporary golf course has its benchmark in Ellerston and in both cases the rest simply do not compare with the best.

The dramatic fairway bunkering of the long par five 9th hole.

The National Golf Club, Moonah Course

Course opened: 2000
Designers: Greg Norman, Bob Harrison

If God did not want man to play golf, he wouldn't have left us land like this.

Situated on the spectacular seaside farmlands of Victoria's Mornington Peninsula, the National Golf Club's Moonah Course is a modern treasure. Like a links but unlike anything we've seen in this country, the course was built on breathtaking coastal dune land and gets its name from the indigenous trees scattered throughout its rugged rolling hills.

The overwhelming beauty of this virgin land, with its stunning rural and ocean panoramas, imposed a responsibility on designers Greg Norman and Bob Harrison to produce something truly exceptional. As Harrison explains: 'There were natural golf holes everywhere and our task was to select the best ones and link them together to form an inspiring and memorable course'. The irregular shape of the site, however, meant routing the course was never going to be easy, with the land taking them to the furthest point from the clubhouse and forcing holes to be laid out in a single loop away from the base.

The team spent hundreds of hours on site developing alternative layouts and considering various combinations to squeeze as many great holes as possible into the routing. To their credit they also ensured the course doesn't suffer from overkill, with the dramatic moments carefully spread and interspersed with a number of more subtle yet equally enjoyable holes.

Pivotal to Moonah's success as a quasi-links was the shaping of fairways, greens and bunkers to not only suit the land but also the fierce Peninsula elements. The choice of grass was vital so the fairways were covered in a common couch known as CT2 that allows the bounce of a links but slows the running ball, thus softening the effect of the rolling contours.

The Cape Schanck winds are a constant factor blowing hard and from opposite directions in summer and winter. Consequently, most of the greens were built with open fronts to accommodate running approach shots. Rather than create Trent Jones-style contouring, the designers chose instead to let their greens follow the flow of the land and included upslopes on many to allow skilled golfers to work the ball back towards more inaccessible pin positions.

The bunkering is outstanding and, aside from some incredible signature holes, is Moonah's most distinguishable feature. Kept smaller than is normal, the hazards were first excavated quite roughly, with the wind then left to blow the sand around before the edges,

Moonah's par three 5th hole.

The wild fairway movement and distant dunes of Moonah's incredible 11th.

and parts of the faces, were seeded with fescues to provide a jagged appearance. This method of construction helped the ungroomed traps blend uniquely into the landscape, striking the perfect balance between looking wild and natural and providing fair and reasonable playing areas.

Also distinctive is the fairway shaping with a series of exhilarating driving holes built among or across the steep ridges. Most fairways have generous width but reward the successful gamble with a shorter and easier approach. The first hole, with its expansive landing area, sets the tone beautifully. Chances are you won't miss the fairway with your opening tee shot, but play too far down the left side and your best chance of par is from one of the greenside traps.

The drive on 3 is an early highlight with a severe fracture cutting across a wide fairway to kick accurate balls towards the target and push weak drives away to leave a difficult approach. The tee shot on the 4th is yet another beauty, this time from atop a large dune out over sweeping undulations. Both greens are also exceptional, the bunkerless 3rd set down in a bowl and the 4th deliciously raised and set naturally within the shape of surrounding mounds.

Other standout holes include fabulous par fours at 10 and 18, a great set of par threes and the highly original 6th with its ocean views and ferocious fairway movement. The par fives are also superb, especially 2, 7 and 15, which rate among the best few modern long holes in Australia.

The most interesting hole, however, is the 11th for a number of reasons, not the least being that the designers were so keen to include this wild countryside that they had to trade off routing difficulties to get to it. Tucked away in the northwest corner of the property, the hole sits beautifully across the undulations with the tee shot, from a ridge to an elevated valley surrounded by sand, one of the genuine highlights of the entire National complex. Equally thrilling is the approach over a hollow towards a punchbowl green framed by the distant Bass Strait dunes. Surrounded by the sounds of a roaring ocean, this is primitive golf at its best.

To balance the use of this extraordinary land, the closing stretch is made up of a series of long holes that head back to the clubhouse and usually into the teeth of the stiff southerly winds. The key to scoring well at Moonah, therefore, is to get through the first eleven holes

without too many scars, as the battle to hold onto your score coming home is one of the toughest, and most exciting, in the country.

There are not many courses in Australia, of any era, as spectacular as Moonah and although it appeals to the masses, for low markers who like their golf raw, this is a special treat. It consequently comes as no surprise to discover this is a course Greg Norman himself is particularly fond of. Prior to construction he described what Mother Nature had left him as 'something that designers drool for', adding that the chance to work with land of such quality was very rare. With the help of a strong design team he did not waste the opportunity, creating a contemporary classic and adding to the lasting legacy he had already left the Australian golfscape.

Part of a long, tough closing stretch, the awesome par five 15th.

Moonah's rugged bunkering, seen here hiding the green on the par three 13th.

Capital Golf Club

Course opened: 1997
Designers: Peter Thomson, Michael Wolveridge, Ross Perrett, Lloyd Williams

'And so it sits, locked away for the exclusive benefit of Lloyd and his friends who love it and cherish it for what it is, simply the best kept secret in Australian golf.'

Michael Wolveridge

Throughout the glorious history of golf course architecture, there have been numerous examples of visionaries who, when struggling to discover golfing perfection, have instead attempted to create it themselves. Most famously, Bobby Jones at Augusta National and George Crump at Pine Valley instantly recognised the world-class potential of their respective sites and refused to rest until the finest golf courses imaginable had been built.

In the modern era, American billionaire Steve Wynn took nature out of the equation by using extravagant modern earth moving techniques to craft his own masterpiece in the flat Nevada desert. Shadow Creek was the course and its success inspired Melbourne businessman and passionate golfer, Lloyd Williams, to indulge a golfing fantasy by attempting to build his own version of golf's classic course.

The Williams vision was to create a true championship layout, free from crowds and distractions, which could challenge the world's best golfers and inspire them with its beauty. The starting point was a modest market garden within the fertile Melbourne Sandbelt. With a seemingly infinite budget, the design was complemented by 35 acres of pristine handcrafted lakes and thriving wildlife reserves complete with emus, wallabies, wild swans and more than 85 species of birds. In excess of 500,000 trees were also planted to create a secluded oasis, transforming the 300-acre site into sacred golfing grounds the equal of almost any on earth.

Opening in 1997, the Capital Golf Club concept was instantly surrounded by mystery. Serene and surreptitious, the course made immediate headlines by attracting high profile clientele and providing fodder for speculative gossip on what lay behind the wrought iron gates and electric security fences. As one of those who have been fortunate to sample the Capital's bounties, I can confirm the worst fears of all lusting golfers—the course is as good as they have imagined.

First the amenities, which are the most lavish in Australia. The magnificent clubhouse is a five-star construction of immense proportions with all the trimmings of a luxury hotel as well as an astonishing collection of photographs from the great courses of the world. The

Capital's terrific closing hole and magnificent clubhouse.

opulent practice facilities are superior to any I've seen, and it's little wonder that the game's leading players choose to warm up here when playing big tournaments in Melbourne.

On course, golfers are truly pampered, starting with enormous tee boxes that are flat enough to satisfy the most sophisticated spirit level and which are surrounded by pristine luma hedges. Gently undulating fairways of pure couch offer impeccable lies and facilitate thrilling approach shots into beautifully contoured bentgrass greens, which run as quick and true as any on the Sandbelt. Designer Peter Thomson makes the point that the Capital's conditioning is almost too good. 'Tees, fairways and greens have a smoothness and quality that touches upon the incredible', he says. 'It seems an act of wanton destruction to take a divot or to march through a white bunker. Putting on the greens is like walking on smooth silk.'

Aside from exceptional playing surfaces, the Capital is also a masterpiece of design. Peter Thomson and Michael Wolveridge were chiefly responsible, although they clearly worked to a detailed Lloyd Williams master plan. Describing the Capital as a fantasy 'which has become a reality', Williams drew inspiration from all corners of the globe and recalled experiences at the world's finest golf courses to help create his unique vision. Of particular interest is the bunkering, which is a mix of the classic Sandbelt style of sprawling bunker and the more traditional shape of the Thomson/Wolveridge pot bunker. The combination works beautifully to create a number of stunning sandy sequences, particularly on the four short holes.

The owner's continued pursuit of perfection and meticulous attention to detail has seen a number of holes tweaked since opening, with all eighteen now leaving an indelible impression on those who play them. The most significant facelift came at the water carry 8th hole when the series of small traps that originally protected the peninsula green were converted into a sandy wasteland. The bunkering was extended to the water's edge and framed by thick clumps of kangaroo grass to form an awesome vista from the tee. This is not the only sublime par three on the course, however, with the equally attractive 16th another highlight.

An accomplished golfer himself, Williams recognised the desire of modern professionals to be constantly stimulated and obliged by building a number of strong back 'Tiger' tees. The par five 7th is a classic example and is as charming and challenging as the hole it is often compared to, the famous 13th at Augusta National. Measuring more than 500 metres,

'In time the course will become acknowledged for what it is—a golfing masterpiece that should stand the test of time and take its place amongst the famous. There may never be another quite like it.'

Peter Thomson

The pitch across the creek to the deliciously back-to-front sloping par five 7th green.

the green is only reachable for the longest hitters who can take on the sand, water and dogleg from the tee and a tantalising creek on the approach. Tiger Woods has hit a six iron into this green while Aaron Baddeley once holed a two iron here for an albatross.

To avoid any semblance of disruption from a bustling outside world, the holes are enclosed by built-up mounds and plant life cleverly positioned to eliminate unattractive views but subtle enough to appear as natural undulation. Aside from protecting the integrity of the course from the prying eyes of unwanted observers, the mounding also gives an amphitheatre backdrop to many greens and fairways.

High rollers from the Melbourne casino and the social and sporting elite including past Presidents of the United States, Prime Ministers of Australia, State Premiers and contemporary golf icons like Tiger Woods, Greg Norman and Sergio Garcia, have all enjoyed the tranquillity of the Capital fairways. While sadly a course solely for the fortunate few, the Capital Golf Club is clearly one of Australia's finest golf experiences.

Always immaculate, the 17th fairway shows off the Capital's contrasting bunker styles.

The Golf Club Kennedy Bay

Course opened: 1999
Designers: Michael Coate, Roger Mackay, Ian Baker-Finch

The final featured modern course is the largely unheralded Kennedy Bay, forty minutes south of Perth. Despite its youth, this is an authentic links, beautifully designed and built in the manner of the most traditional British courses.

Located among the charming sand hills of Port Kennedy and alongside the blue waters of the Indian Ocean, the site is not dissimilar to many of the classic links and is defined by a series of dune ridges and valleys that were formed over a period of 8000 years. Designer Michael Coate explains that the composition of the land and the surrounding sand dunes 'lent itself to the creation of a true British-style links course, utilising the alignments of the ridges and valleys and hanging the greens and tees off the natural formations'. Coate was initially the sole designer, with the developer calling in professional golfer Roger Mackay to help shape the character of the design and Ian Baker-Finch to advise during the course's construction.

The routing at Kennedy Bay sensibly follows the natural flow of the land, as holes weave in and around the wonderful dunes. Lined by coastal scrub and fescue roughs, the fast fairways offer tight lies and promote the use of running approach shots into large,

The opening hole, and the first of more than 100 pot bunkers you'll meet at Kennedy Bay.

undulating greens which are protected by swales and steep mounds. More than 100 small pot bunkers are used throughout the course without a single trap being wasted. Traditionally shaped and built with revetted faces, those not in play because of wind conditions either act as sighters from the tee or are positioned simply to encourage the gamble.

The purity of this ancient links experience and collective strength of the design can be overwhelming, and upon further reflection it is actually surprising just how many first-class holes the course boasts.

Clever fairway bunkering on the 9th pushes most tee shots to the right leaving a longer, more difficult approach.

There are highlights everywhere, with the most outstanding being the attractive double act at the 15th and 16th holes. The par four 15th moves slightly right with its fairway set across the tee presenting an awesome risk/reward driving challenge over sand or scrub, depending on the wind and your level of bravado. The 16th is a gorgeous hole and the pick of an excellent set of par threes. Referred to as 'Wee Tap' and measuring little more than 130 metres, the hole can play anything from a wedge to four iron depending on the sea breezes. Protected by front and back pot bunkers, the delicious green is elevated, tilted across the hole and less than 10 metres deep.

The short par fours are superb, especially the driveable 7th with its raised target guarded by sharp contouring and an ingenious trap that eats into the left side of the enormous green to catch those who get 'too cute' with their pitch. Also exceptional are the longer par fours with most cleverly named to invoke a sense for the challenge they present. The 'Coate Hanger' 9th is a great example, with a ring of pot bunkers in the corner of the dogleg forcing the timid to drive wide on the fairway and further from the green. The 'Split Decision' 11th is another well named hole, with its ideal driving line down a tight left side flanked by bunkers, while the safer right side is more open but leaves an approach over sand and slopes.

Like any truly great links, the region's coastal breeze, known as the 'Fremantle Doctor', is the course's greatest defence as it swings around and strengthens in the afternoons. Indeed, to fully appreciate the Kennedy Bay experience, you need to spend a full day there tackling the links in the relative calm of an early morning and then heading out again in the stiff afternoon winds to fight desperately for the pars which had earlier been birdies.

Although the course lacks the real dirty weather, its design, dunes, undulation, tight surfaces and constant buffeting from the 'Fremantle Doctor' give an authentic Scottish feel, with only the temperate climate to remind you this is in fact Western Australia.

Unfortunately Kennedy Bay has been dogged by management problems that date back to its opening in May 1999. The course was closed within a month and stayed shut for more than a year, before reopening in early 2001 to belated acclaim. Despite the quality of the product, a string of companies have been unable to make the operation profitable, as the Perth golfing public have failed to support a course they should feel immensely proud of. Western Australia, with its tremendous variety, is certainly an underrated golf destination, but take a great track like Kennedy Bay out of the mix and things suddenly seem a little lean. This was the prospect the industry faced when the course lay idle, unwanted and unkempt, and though now resurrected, it is still to be fully embraced.

Though word is slowly spreading, Kennedy Bay remains the most incredible hidden gem we have in this country, and in many ways it's a shame the links is located on the West Coast of Australia when clearly the golfers who will enjoy this layout the most reside on the East.

Those who have played Kennedy Bay do not need to be told how good it is, but for those who are yet to make the trip my advice is to do so quickly, before the locals realise how good it is and take all the tee times.

The 2nd green, one of several raised targets at Kennedy Bay.

VICTORIA

Although the first ball was struck in Tasmania and the first club formed in New South Wales, Australian golf's spiritual home is Victoria. The history of the game in this country is inextricably tied not only to the state but also the 1891 birth of our greatest golf club, Royal Melbourne. Prior to its momentous shift to the southern Sandbelt, the club hosted the nation's first professional match and first men's amateur championship, and also became the first in Australia to be granted the 'Royal' prefix.

The discovery of the club's Sandringham site and subsequent move inspired other clubs to seek out similar sandy golfing grounds and the Melbourne Sandbelt was born. By the end of the 1920s, the city's major clubs had established themselves within the Sandbelt and the area subsequently developed into arguably the finest and most recognisable golf region on Earth.

The most significant episode in the development of the game within Victoria was, of course, the visit of Dr Alister MacKenzie in 1926. While in town he designed the brilliant West Course at Royal Melbourne, consulted at several other Melbourne tracks and trained the two men, Alex Russell and Mick Morcom, who would continue his legacy after he departed. The success of the entire area is a tribute to the skills of these three incredible men.

While the Sandbelt continues to boast Australia's greatest concentration of world-class courses, the gap over its rivals has narrowed significantly during the modern era, with the Mornington Peninsula rapidly developing into an awesome destination in its own right. Within an hour of the Melbourne clubs, the Peninsula features the same plentiful supply of sand and an outstanding selection of courses mostly built since the early 1990s. Completing the triumvirate of great golf in and around Melbourne is the Bellarine Peninsula, on the western side of Port Philip Bay, popular for its quaint coastal communities and two wonderful courses at Barwon Heads.

With so much great golf within arm's reach of city golfers, other gems scattered throughout the state like Horsham, Port Fairy, Lakes Entrance, Warrnambool and the Murray River courses are easily overlooked. As Peter Thomson once explained, 'it is possible in Victoria to indulge oneself in golfing fare to the point of gluttony'.

Previous spread: The National Golf Club, Moonah Course 2nd hole.

Below: Victorian golf's sacred site —Royal Melbourne— from behind the 2nd green on the East Course.

The Melbourne Sandbelt

The Royal Melbourne Golf Club, East Course

Course opened: 1932
Designer: Alex Russell

The concept for the Royal Melbourne East Course was born shortly after Alister MacKenzie had left Australia and while his famous West Course was still under construction. The club's plan to build a new clubhouse on the current 7th West was well advanced when two parcels of land east of the main Black Rock site became available in 1929. The prospect of 36 holes appealed to the membership who decided to proceed with the second course and shelve plans to relocate the clubhouse, permanently as it would turn out.

While designing the West Course, MacKenzie had also mapped an alternative nine hole layout, which was made redundant when the additional land for the East Course was purchased. With MacKenzie back in the United States his new partner, Alex Russell, was put in charge of the design and interestingly decided to lay his first four holes along the lines suggested as part of this shorter course. Aside from the shape of these holes, however, only the first actually resembles MacKenzie's original plan.

The very nature and distribution of the available land meant that the East Course would differ considerably from the West. Holes are played in a single loop away from the clubhouse, across several roads and covering three separate allotments. Despite the obstacles and inferior terrain of the eastern property, Russell's routing works surprisingly well with balanced nines and a great variety of holes. Sensibly, the long holes tackle the wind from each direction, while the only minor criticism of his arrangement is that all four wonderful par threes play to the north.

The East Course's brilliant Russell/MacKenzie-designed short par four opening hole.

Club greenkeeper Mick Morcom was used to build the course, again proving himself to be Australian golf's master shaper. His bunkering is superb while the greens, though smaller than the West's, are as beautifully constructed and intricately sloped.

The East Course starts and finishes on the main site alongside its more famous sibling, with these seven 'home paddock' holes the highlight. Incorporating the most dramatic undulation on the course, the short four, long four, mid four start is brilliant, with clear risk/reward options from the tee and birdie to double bogey possibilities. The closing stretch is equally memorable starting, with the short par four 15th and the heavily bunkered 16th, which is the flattest 'home paddock' hole of either course and one of the best and most underrated par threes in Melbourne.

The final two holes, famously used as the climax to the world-renowned Composite course, are also exceptional with 18 one of the most awesome finishing holes in golf.

The Composite course was first conceived in 1959 when the club played host to the Canada Cup (now World Cup). Using twelve holes from the West and six from the East, the tournament propelled Royal Melbourne onto the global stage. It also highlighted the quality of Russell's work, with his all-star holes standing comfortably alongside MacKenzie's and blending into one outstanding layout.

Despite the occasional configuration adjustment, neither group of holes has changed greatly since inception. On the East Course, the 17th was lengthened prior to the 1959 event and cross bunkers moved closer to the green. Later the 3rd tee was built up so the once blind fairway would be visible from the tee and local boys thus dissuaded from snatching golf balls. Otherwise, with the exception of some minor bunker adjustments, the course has survived virtually intact, a tribute to Russell's classic design.

Royal Melbourne's East Course is often unfairly rated because of the esteemed company it keeps, yet any track with holes the quality of the first four and final four is certainly very special. There are many other highlights as well, including the cross bunkering on the 10th and the approach through the saddle of sand at the difficult 12th. Although the disparity between the best and worst holes, and best and worst land, prevents East from outranking West, to my mind only a handful of Australian courses boast anywhere near its number of genuinely world-class moments.

After the good doctor departed our shores Russell was a man in demand, kept busy overseeing the MacKenzie projects and completing work of his own. Despite a flurry of design activity, the East Course remains his masterpiece, fitting therefore that it should stand alongside the greatest accomplishment of his illustrious mentor.

The Victoria Golf Club

Course opened: 1927
Designers: William Meader, Oscar Damman, Dr Alister MacKenzie

Melbourne businessman William Meader is considered the forefather of Victorian golf, having helped establish the state's Golf Association in 1902 and founding the Victoria Golf Club at Fishermen's Bend the following year. Meader was later the driving force behind the move to Cheltenham and in 1923, with club captain Oscar Damman, laid out the current course. Construction was hampered, however, by bad weather and problems with site access, but the delay proved a blessing as it allowed travelling architect Dr Alister MacKenzie to advise on the bunkering of the unfinished course.

Clearly impressed, MacKenzie told the club that 'little more is required to make this a magnificent golf course', and then proceeded to add finishing touches to the existing routing by mapping bunkers and suggesting a few green changes.

Victoria's 'fine drive and pitch' 10th hole.

Perfectly situated in the heart of the Melbourne Sandbelt and across the road from Royal Melbourne, the layout these three men created is outstanding, with a collection of fine holes falling beautifully across the naturally undulating terrain. Fairways are forgiving yet place a premium on preferred driving lines while the green sites are brilliantly contoured and original. The style of design together with the shape of MacKenzie's bold bunkering, the slope of the land and use of native vegetation is somewhat reminiscent of Royal Melbourne, albeit on a slightly smaller scale.

The central and southern sections of the site are the highlight, particularly holes 9 through 13, which take the golfer on an absorbing journey through the most interesting undulation on the course. The long 9th is a classic Sandbelt par five running across the tumbling hills while the wonderful short 10th, described by MacKenzie in 1926 as 'a fine drive and pitch adventure', features a dipping, sweeping fairway and sublime green site.

The 4th hole and the first of four very good par threes at Victoria.

Falling away towards the southwestern corner of the property, the charming 12th finishes little more than a wedge from Royal Melbourne and is followed by the best par four on the course, which heads blind over a rise and then into an elevated green from a down-sloping fairway.

Many believe Victoria's greatest weakness is the configuration of holes as each nine closes with back-to-back par fives. Despite being an unusual arrangement, the 9th and 17th are both world-class, while the famous short 18th provides a stirring finish with many matches decided on its enormous front-to-back sloping green. Like most holes at Victoria, gaping MacKenzie sand traps strategically line the approach to the green and dominate the vista from the top of the fairway.

Although some play down MacKenzie's influence at Victoria, it is impossible to deny that his superb bunkers define the character of the course. Identifying a weakness in the Australian game, MacKenzie actually boasted during his visit that his scheme of bunkering would help raise the standard of golf by 'stimulating the scratch man to improve his game'. This prophecy was most famously realised at Victoria, which began producing champion golfers almost the moment he departed.

During the 1980s one such member, five-time British Open champion Peter Thomson, was responsible for one of the only significant course changes when he raised the green on the driveable 1st hole. More recently the club sought to regenerate the layout after years of slow deterioration by employing local architect Michael Clayton to oversee the renovation of the original bunkering. Referring back to an old black and white aerial shot of the course taken shortly after the 1927 opening, Clayton expertly and faithfully restored the famous MacKenzie hazards to their former glory.

Careful to preserve the subtlety and integrity of the original design, some minor tweaking also took place in preparation for the 2002 Australian Open. A number of holes, 5, 9, 17 and 18, were lengthened and alterations made to strengthen the par five finishing holes. The bunkering and mounding around the 17th green was reworked significantly while the 18th tee was extended, the landing area tightened and greenside bunkers enhanced. These modern changes were relatively minor and have been generally well received.

Long regarded as one of our elite courses, Victoria today exists as a tribute to the hard-working pioneers who laid the clubs foundations, and the divine contribution of Dr MacKenzie who helped shape a very good golf club into a truly great one.

The Metropolitan Golf Club

Course opened: 1908
Designers: J.B. Mackenzie, Dr Alister MacKenzie, Dick Wilson

The second oldest golf club in the Sandbelt, Metropolitan's founding members were originally part of Royal Melbourne when the club golfed on a leased estate near the Caulfield railway station. Fearing for the future of their links, the majority of members moved to a permanent home at Sandringham, while those for whom the Caulfield course was more accessible remained. A few years later, these 'stay at home' members purchased the Barholme Estate in Oakleigh and relocated as The Metropolitan Golf Club.

The chosen site was farmland with less natural undulation than Royal Melbourne, but the same fertile sandy base found throughout Melbourne's Sandbelt region. Initially lacking feature, decades of maturation and shrewd club management saw the flat countryside famously transformed into a site of regal and botanical beauty, boasting an impeccable golf course of international significance.

Engineer member J.B. Mackenzie laid out the first course, with his routing taking advantage of the unusual shape of the estate by including several fine doglegs and fairways that ran in a number of directions. The design was complemented by magnificent plantings of Australian native trees and shrubs, which remain Metropolitan's most distinguishable feature. His most celebrated hole was the old par four 14th, described by Gene Sarazen in 1936 as 'one of golf's best'.

With seven of the first nine holes continuing to play along the lines he laid out, J.B. Mackenzie is considered the club's spiritual father. The final two holes are also close to his originals, although the 17th was shifted slightly east when the course was rearranged during the 1960s, which brought the now famous row of swamp cypresses into play for the first time.

Metropolitan's 17th hole with its infamous swamp cypresses guarding the right side of the fairway.

The other MacKenzie, Dr Alister, also had a major hand in the design of Metropolitan, advising on possible course improvements during his 1926 visit to Melbourne. His principal observations were that the bunkering lacked strategy and had not been positioned close enough to the greens. He also suggested some minor routing changes. MacKenzie's influence on the current course should not be understated, as aside from designing the brilliant bunkering and altering some of the greens, he also moved the first tee to create an outstanding dogleg, and shifted the 9th green back to its present location.

Sadly, with the exception of the final two holes and the tee shot on the 10th, none of the other back nine holes is arranged as either Mackenzie had intended. American Dick Wilson rebuilt these holes in 1960, when the rapid expansion of the surrounding residential community forced the club to sell their beloved southern holes for a local school development. Fortunately, the club managed to purchase a tongue of market garden that extended into its original site and Wilson was able to skilfully design seven new holes to blend into the established course. The only distinguishable differences are minor aesthetic contrasts between the bunkering. Though classics like the old 14th could not be duplicated, he did build a superb long par four at the 15th, while the 16th, with its abundance of sand, has become one of the highlights.

Following this period of upheaval came a resolve within the club to re-establish the course as one of the nation's best, with the focus shifting towards improving the playing surfaces. Their success has been extraordinary, especially since the early 1990s, with Metropolitan now revered both locally and internationally as having some of the finest golfing turf on the planet.

Aside from immaculate grooming, the tree-lined fairways also provide a constant feeling of seclusion and isolation on virtually every hole. As far back as 1926, the beauty of the site was undeniable, even moving the well-travelled Dr MacKenzie to comment that 'no remarks upon the Metropolitan Club would be complete without reference to the magnificent plantations. From a field, plain, unattractive and lacking beauty in the first place, it has been transformed into its present state of sylvan glory. Metropolitan members certainly take their golf in beautiful surroundings'.

Decades of additional growth and the sensible fine tuning of the exceptional three-man design has furthered this experience and surpassed what either pioneering Mackenzie could have reasonably imagined during the club's formative years. The modern Metropolitan membership is truly one of the most spoilt in Australia.

The 18th green and surrounds with the faultless playing surfaces typical of the Metropolitan experience.

Commonwealth Golf Club

Course opened: 1921
Designers: Sam Bennett, Charles Lane, Sloan Morpeth

Commonwealth was formed in 1920 when members of the Waverley Golf Club, looking to move to the prospering Sandbelt, purchased the club's current site close to the Metropolitan Golf Club. Inaugural professional, Sam Bennett, designed the initial twelve holes before club captain and budding amateur architect, Charles Lane, finished off the eighteen. Lane also touched up the greens and was even seen during construction digging some of the famous greenside bunkers. Unusually for its vintage, the course then evolved primarily without the aid of high profile, high price golf course architects, but instead thanks to the long history of sound internal club management.

What club pioneers created was extraordinary and based around the strict adherence to the simplest values of strategic design. Beautifully bunkered and exquisitely contoured, the titled greens are designed to reward players who can approach from the best angles. Accordingly, the fairways were shaped and designed to create clear choices from the tee according to one's ability.

This design philosophy is best highlighted on the superb par fours, the classic example being the famous 16th. The hole shapes left around a fairway lake with a slippery green guarded by a fearsome right side bunker. The angle of the green rewards the brave golfer who can drive close to the water with a much easier approach free from the menacing bunker.

Another standout, the mid-length par four 11th, is played around corner bunkers and sweeps uphill towards a large tiered green, with a steep slope and deep bunkering. The final two holes are also outstanding and form part of a much-celebrated closing stretch.

Commonwealth's signature hole, the strategic 16th.

Following the world class 16th is an exceptional short par four, which rises gently to a delicious green with sharp contours. The overzealous beware, as pitch shots in from the wrong angle here are devilishly difficult. The 18th, with its modern length and classical bunkering, is an excellent finish to the round and the scene of many last hole heroics.

For many decades the members acted as custodians of their course, successfully able to maintain the integrity of its timeless design in-house. The greatest period of reform came during the 1960s when additional land allowed long-time club Secretary Sloan Morpeth to redesign the 10th and 11th holes as well as a number of green sites. These Morpeth changes, together with additional alterations by subsequent committees, enhanced the experience and helped the course develop its distinct character.

In recent times this very character was threatened when technological advancements and increased competition were thought to have rendered the layout obsolete. The club abandoned its internal management policy and instead embarked on a program to modernise the course. First came the loss of the beloved driveable opening hole, which was fondly remembered but underweight according to a committee who added length and created a dogleg. Architect Kevin Hartley then built a new par three in the 1990s to replace the popular short 7th hole and made further alterations which added a total of 200 metres to the length of the course. An extensive tree planting program was also continued, which has yielded a beautiful collection of native flora but has also caused problems with intruding limbs interfering with the line of play on several holes.

The contemporary Commonwealth is still an incredible golf course, despite these modern changes affecting the flow of holes and doing little to improve the experience. There remains a stack of wonderful moments, world-class holes on both sides, and the original greens and bunkers are still as strategic and attractive as any on the Sandbelt.

Commonwealth's continued success can be directly attributed to the design philosophies implemented by the club's early members, and although some recent alterations appear out of character, any analysis of today's course stirs great passion among a justifiably proud membership. Indeed, if one can ignore fond reflection and examine what 'still is' rather than remember what 'once was', then the course measures up favourably against most in Australia.

Revered internationally yet often chastised locally, Commonwealth remains an icon of the Sandbelt and one of our foremost classic courses.

Woodlands Golf Club

Course opened: 1913
Designers: R.S. Banks, S. Bennett

Largely unheralded outside of Melbourne, the Woodlands Golf Club is yet another exceptional example of classic Australian golf course architecture within the glorious Sandbelt.

Teacher and fanatical golfer George Rogers found the site while visiting the adjacent Epsom racecourse to seek permission to hit golf balls around the racetrack. The land was part of the stately Mayfield Estate and Rogers, with the help of some keen golf friends who were knocking balls around an old railway paddock, managed to convince the trustees to lease part of its grounds for golf.

Founded in 1913 as the Mordialloc Golf Club, members initially golfed on a nine hole course laid out by Albert Park professional Rowley Banks. As the popularity of the course grew additional land was allocated to the club, and in 1917 a further nine holes, this time designed by club Professional Sam Bennett, were opened.

Evolving considerably in the early days, the course has remained largely unchanged since the 1920s when the classic 7th hole was redeveloped and the bunkering added under the watchful eye of Royal Melbourne Greenkeeper Mick Morcom. Prior to Morcom building his famous bunkers, turning earth on the estate had been forbidden and the club was instead forced to use portable wire netting as hazards in place of actual bunkers.

Short by today's standards, Woodlands is no pushover, with tight tree-lined fairways and a clever mix of outstanding short holes and testing, intelligent longer holes. The greens,

The sun sets on Woodlands' wonderful 7th hole.

which get notoriously firm and fast in summer, have their own unique character and are the course's main defence against low scoring. Small and elevated, they are protected by strategically positioned bunkers, banks, humps and hollows. Hitting the tiny targets in regulation means plenty of great birdie opportunities, which is why good iron players particularly enjoy this course.

Despite a number of tremendous holes, it's the four exceptional short par fours that stand out. Three are driveable, while the fabulous mid-length 7th hole is a drive and pitch to one of the most unique greens in marvellous Melbourne. Each has a distinct character, attacks the wind from a different angle and offers a number of options for players of any level from the tee. Other course highlights include the bunkering on the 5th and 15th, tough back-to-back par fours at the 9th and 10th, and the frightfully tight 17th which is only short but has one of the toughest greens to hit of any par three on the Sandbelt.

Although not an easy course to score well at, the great variety at Woodlands makes it one of our most enjoyable classic courses. The playing surfaces are always superb and the bunker restoration undertaken in recent years has been a tremendous success, with the bunkering now being the equal to courses like Commonwealth and Metropolitan, and only marginally inferior to the much lauded hazards at Kingston Heath and Royal Melbourne.

Woodlands pre-dates Alister MacKenzie's visit to Australia and came of age during the Golden era that he inspired, yet despite retaining the characteristics that make Sandbelt golf so wonderful, the lack of the great man's insignia has seen the course perennially underrated.

Beautifully bunkered, the 15th is one of the Sandbelt's premier par fives.

Yarra Yarra Golf Club

Course opened: 1928
Designer: Alex Russell

Like most of the major Melbourne Sandbelt clubs, Yarra Yarra was born many miles away from the fertile golfing ground it currently calls home. Originally the Eaglemont Golf Club, the name Yarra Yarra was adopted when a move to Rosanna, along the banks of Melbourne's Yarra River, was made in 1898.

In the 1920s, with the increasing popularity of the southern Sandbelt region, came the realisation that if the club wanted to retain members and receive championship credentials it would have to move where the sand was plentiful and the game was booming. An emergency meeting of members, convened toward the end of 1926, endorsed the committee's decision to seek a new home close to the recently relocated, and thriving, Commonwealth Golf Club.

They picked a great location and an opportune time to move, with the Alister MacKenzie-trained Alex Russell able to design the layout and oversee its construction, for a nominal fee, as part of his architectural education. Russell believed the land at Yarra was superior to that at Metropolitan, Commonwealth and Kingston Heath and told members that it would be possible to make 'the finest golfing course you could ever see on the land'. Dr MacKenzie, who had never seen the site, apparently used surveyor's plans of the property to assist with the design by sending rudimentary sketches and ideas for Russell to implement. Little evidence of this input remains, however, and it would be unfair to deny Russell the credit for the finished product.

The superb greens and bunkers are the highlight at Yarra and are as good as many of MacKenzie's own creations. Typically large, fast and undulating, the greens feature some of the most extreme slopes in Melbourne, while the bunkers are constructed to blend naturally with their surrounds and are intrinsic to the strategy of each hole. Throughout Victoria, the

One of Yarra Yarra's world famous par threes, the 4th hole, though softened over the years, still demands a pinpoint approach.

The classic Sandbelt bunkering on the approach to the risk/ reward par five 9th.

best bunkers and greens remain those either designed by MacKenzie or built by the men he trained, and Yarra's are up there with the very best.

The par threes are world-renowned with the incredible 11th hole among the top few short holes in the country. Its notorious target is heavily bunkered and tilted across you from the tee with two tiers, four shelves and a heavy slope from the back. Any two-putt from above this hole is worthy of wild celebration. The natural subtleties of the land are also used to great effect, with a number of outstanding driving holes, the best example being the par four 5th with its crested fairway dipping and rising again towards a large sloping green visible from the tee. The bunkering of the last third of this hole is quite brilliant.

Though the design of each hole has evolved through the generations, the routing has remained essentially untouched. Early committees made the most significant changes when they planted rows of pines, wattles, gums and eucalypts to line fairways and define the holes. In more recent times, some minor changes were needed to protect neighbouring properties, while a few greens, most noticeably the 4th and 8th, have been slightly reshaped. Among the more interesting on the course, the steep slopes on these two greens were sadly softened to allow the club additional pin positions.

MacKenzie, who so enjoyed the beautiful surroundings at Metropolitan, would have no doubt appreciated Yarra Yarra, which features a similarly attractive setting of indigenous and imported plantings. Though the site is much more confined than Metropolitan and sixteen holes run in a north–south direction, the tremendous variety of design makes up for any shortcomings. Aside from the previously mentioned 5th and 11th holes, other classic Sandbelt moments include short par threes at the 4th and 15th and the long par four 13th. The risk/reward par fives are also memorable, with the tight 9th fairway slanted towards a series of bunkers and requiring two brave shots to reach a huge green, while the delicate 16th is easily reachable for the modern golfer but protected by menacing cross bunkers.

As a regular tournament venue since the 1950s, Yarra is famously remembered as the scene of Gary Player's first professional victory in the Ampol tournament way back in 1956.

The Peninsula Country Golf Club, North Course

Course opened: 1969
Designers: Sloan Morpeth, Michael Clayton

The Peninsula Country Golf Club is one of our best golfing facilities, with two excellent courses beautifully positioned geographically within the Melbourne Sandbelt, yet only minutes from the thriving Mornington Peninsula.

Peninsula was originally founded as an eleven hole course in 1924 and had extended to 27 holes before embarking on a significant move during the 1950s in an attempt to elevate itself into the elite upper echelon of Australian golf. The club acquired an adjacent site and engaged Melbourne golf identity, Sloan Morpeth, to design and oversee the building of the North and South courses. Morpeth was able to incorporate twelve of the existing holes into the new design of the South Course, while the North Course was new and built on superbly undulating, sandy high ground with the odd view out to Melbourne's Port Phillip Bay.

The two courses were always clearly distinguishable. The South had championship length and difficulty, was highly rated and a regular venue for leading amateur events. The North, on the other hand, was a shorter, quirky course built on more dramatic land yet less regarded because of its unconventional design.

At the close of the 20th century, with their courses slipping down ranking lists, the board decided to radically upgrade facilities, including a major revision of all 36 holes. Local tournament professional turned designer Michael Clayton was commissioned to produce a master plan and oversee the changes to both courses. The result of work done to the North Course in 2002 was nothing short of remarkable and transformed the little course with infinite potential into the new darling of the Melbourne Sandbelt.

No longer the standout, Peninsula's South Course still has several wonderful holes such as the one shot 14th.

A thrilling driving hole, the fairway on the 8th beautifully follows the North Course's natural shape.

Using the natural topography, Clayton brilliantly incorporated added areas of native vegetation, natural sandy waste and classic Sandbelt-style bunkering. Although the routing was not significantly altered, he built some superb 'new' golf holes along existing lines and created a number of spectacular vistas, especially on holes 12 and 14. The wild unkempt appearance of the heathland grasses that line fairways and greens is stunning and stirs memories of its more famous Sandbelt cousins. Indeed, there is now as much of Royal Melbourne and Kingston Heath in this course as original Peninsula North.

Challenging with subtlety rather than length, the par threes all run in different directions, while the short to medium par fours bend both ways and slope up, down and across the tumbling dunes. This endless variety is the track's greatest asset with the challenge of each hole altering considerably with Melbourne's changing winds.

Although the front nine is built on the more dramatic land, the highlight for me actually comes towards the close with a fantastic stretch of golf from the 12th through 15th. The tough 12th is a beautifully bunkered medium-length uphill par four with a hogsback fairway lined on the left by a sandy hazard that runs the length of the hole. An exquisite reachable par four follows with its perilous hourglass-shaped green tiny, tiered and difficult to hit if approached from the wrong angle.

An oasis of sand from tee to green dominates the short 14th, which received the most remarkable facelift of any hole on the course. Its wide, sloping green is built into a sizeable sand dune, framed by sublime bunkers and somewhat reminiscent of the famous 5th at Royal Melbourne West. Completing a super set of golf is the long rolling par five 15th, its cross bunkering creating a glorious sandy vista on the approach to the green.

Aside from Royal Melbourne, the North Course land is as good as any in Melbourne and the original design, though a little primitive, had always used the wild movement and native vegetation to great effect. Thanks to Clayton, however, the course feels born-again, with his commonsense tweaking a welcome relief for golfers constantly battered by the classic course striving to be longer and tougher.

For so long tarred with a 'potentially good' epithet, the modern Peninsula North is great fun, wonderfully original and now a true Sandbelt highlight.

The Mornington Peninsula

The Dunes Golf Links
Course opened: 1997
Designer: Tony Cashmore

The fertile linksland of The Dunes was originally occupied by the Limestone Valley Golf Club, a modest, partially-built course set amidst the glorious sand hills of Victoria's Mornington Peninsula. When the club fell into financial ruin, its liquidators decided to sell the entire 240 acres at public auction, and though the land was seemingly bequeathed to golfers, had it not been for a $300 bad debt, the site would have been lost to the golf world forever.

Entrepreneur Duncan Andrews was a small creditor of the ill-fated club, and when informed of the impending sale, his idle curiosity led him to the site. It was never his intention or ambition to build a golf course, but an overwhelming reaction to his first look at the land led to the idea of The Dunes. The existing course was primitive, with holes played through the tumbling hills and valleys with little shaping, few bunkers and modest greens. Aside from the views and the challenge of Man versus Mother Nature, there was little to attract golfers. Andrews though recalls standing on what is now the 17th tee, looking out over the stunning topography and thinking 'God almighty' as he contemplated its potential. He acquired the property in 1994 and appointed Tony Cashmore to undertake a full course redesign.

Cashmore transformed the land into a world-class golf course by modifying existing shapes and devising new ones to blend holes into a seamless golfscape. Despite a wild appearance, the land actually included several dull sections with significant earthworks undertaken on holes 5, 6, 12, 14 and 15 to ensure a visual continuity. Indeed, it would surprise many visitors to learn that some of the most natural looking undulations on these holes including the controversial mound fronting the par three 6th green, are actually hand-crafted Cashmore originals.

The strength of The Dunes is the sum of its parts, with eighteen strong holes and few, if any, indifferent moments. It's actually hard to nominate a hole that doesn't have great visual interest because, as Cashmore explains, 'the land either yielded natural golf vistas, or was deliberately fashioned to excite the golfer's eye from the moment he arrives at the tee'. Despite the apparent challenge, the course is not overly severe for the average player and, remarkably, hole after hole, good scoring is possible. This, he adds, was a deliberate design intention.

'The essential quality of The Dunes is in the variety of its settings, the broad driving spaces, and the constantly changing character of the golf holes, linked seamlessly as a golf journey which you wish would never end.'
Tony Cashmore

The par three 17th at The Dunes is, as Tom Watson described, an 'exquisite golf hole'.

Looking toward the 12th green from the 'natural' sandy waste area that Cashmore created.

The fine collection of par threes is probably shaded by the unique set the team built at Thirteenth Beach, but includes the wonderful 17th which is just about the most naturally beautiful golf hole on the Peninsula. The par fives are also very good, especially the 5th and 12th, which is the designer's favourite hole and totally unrecognisable from the flat terrain it was constructed over. Other highlights include the stretch of left bending holes from the 8th through 10th, the exquisite 4th hole with its tiny green perched atop a ledge, and the attractive valley drive down the 18th fairway.

Though not a links in the strictest sense, the generous fairways set in valleys between dunes with soft jumbled ridges and swales give the course a genuine ancient flavour. A number of greens built in attractive hollows counter those on the gentle ridges, and with the wild bunkering and strong coastal winds, help to complete the links-like experience.

It took the Andrews passion to conceive The Dunes and the Cashmore skill to bring his vision to life. The men spent endless evenings together devouring bottles of wine as they studied contour maps and considered the various combination of holes. The marketing says that 'God made it and we just mow it', but in fact God left a thousand holes and the key for the designer was finding the best fit.

Early morning on the opening hole at the immensely popular and enjoyable Dunes Golf Links.

The Dunes is one of those very rare courses that help define an era with its critical and popular success spawning a series of like styled developments. Though it opened amid the modern boom, this fully public links helped to popularise a region and rekindled interest in an entire genre of golf design.

The National Golf Club, Old Course

Course opened: 1987
Designer: Robert Trent Jones Jr

Australia's largest private golf facility, The National Golf Club, began as a pipe dream in the early 1980s when Melbourne entrepreneur David Inglis decided to build an exclusive golf club in the rugged Cape Schanck hills overlooking Bass Strait. Golf had been played on the remote locale for more than a decade and the Inglis plan was to redesign the financially stricken Cape Country Club course for members and add a further 18 holes for public players.

Wanting an overseas designer to build the new courses, The National initially had a commitment from Pete Dye which fell through when Dye refused to travel to Australia to see the site first hand. Other designers were considered but American Robert Trent Jones Jr was eventually selected, mostly on the back of his great work at Joondalup in Western Australia.

Upon first inspection of the site Trent Jones was blown away by its potential and enthused that 'any golf course architect would kill for a piece of land like this. It is one of the most unique areas of links country left anywhere in the world'. His master plan for The National required the total demolition of the existing course and the introduction of a prestigious residential estate within the club's boundaries, with the land sales helping to fund the project.

Built on a hillside 80 metres above sea level, the course was dramatically crafted through the rugged coastal tea-tree and offers stunning ocean views on sixteen of the holes. These stirring views, together with the constant battle against the harsh Cape Schanck elements, define the experience, with The National 'a lion in the wind or a lamb on a clear sunny day' according to Trent Jones.

Critics of the course tend to find the sharp bunkering, tiered landing areas and thick scrub surrounding the fairways a little too penal, especially in all too frequent high winds. Members, though, enjoy a wry smile when their beloved course is criticised as most that leave apparently unsatisfied with the severity of the challenge, invariably supplicate members for a return game. It's my guess that detractors have only played the course as a lion and never enjoyed it as a lamb during the magically calm, clear Peninsula days when the birdie chances are flowing.

'The National will make me famous—either as the designer who has created one of the world's great golf courses or a designer who stuffed up some of the best golf course real estate imaginable.'

Robert Trent Jones Jr

Out of this world, the National's awesome 7th hole.

To fully appreciate the genius of the Trent Jones design and understand its idiosyncrasies, the course has to be played several times and in a range of weather conditions. The slippery greens are probably Australia's most extreme and can take years to master, with the sharp ridges, steep tiers and frightening speeds making putting adventures both exhilarating and soul destroying at the same time. Indeed: 'Before you putt from the roof of a Volkswagen and try to stop the ball on its bonnet, you should practice on the greens at The National!'

The spectacular par three 7th is the absolute highlight of the course and perhaps the entire Peninsula. From the tee the view extends past the outcrop green site to the crashing waves of Bass Strait, along the Peninsula and even out to Melbourne's Port Philip Bay and city skyline on clear mornings. Played with anything from a wedge to a two iron, the tee shot must carry a wild jagged ravine and land softly on a wonderfully built green almost 80 metres wide but only a few metres deep. Anything short, long or wide here is dead but everything else is fine! If you have never played the hole it is worth travelling from wherever you read this review just to experience this breathtaking work of art.

When the club expanded to 54 holes, a new centralised clubhouse, built to accommodate golfers from each course, forced the reconfiguration of Old Course holes and considerably altered its character. The terrifying 14th, 15th and 16th became the opening holes, and though built to test players coming home they can now destroy the scorecard before the golfer has even warmed up.

The exhilarating outlooks from virtually every corner of this course are a powerful reminder of golf's ability to stimulate the senses. Now referred to as the 'Old' course, 'Original' would have been an equally appropriate caption, so unique is the experience. While the visionaries did a wonderful job building a thriving club so far from a major city, it remains Trent Jones Jr who put The National on the map with a brilliant golf course, unlike any other in the world.

More Trent Jones magic at the partially-blind par three 16th.

Portsea Golf Club

Course opened: 1926
Designer: Jock Young, Sloan Morpeth, Michael Clayton

'What a magnificent golf links this country would make.' Arthur Relph.

Describing the undulating coastal sand dunes that bordered the Point Nepean National Park at Portsea, club founder Arthur Relph in 1923 identified the ideal site with which to build the new Portsea Golf Club.

After securing the land in 1924, Relph commissioned Scottish professional Jock Young to map out the first nine holes and oversee the clearing of the dense scrub, which took fifteen men almost twelve months. The club opened in 1926 and quickly built upon its early foundations with a 10th hole added just two months later and twelve in play by 1932. In 1965, the course was finally extended to 18 holes by Sloan Morpeth and head greenkeeper Jack Howard. Though several green sites and fairways were retained, the 18 Morpeth holes were all originals.

Quite literally carved out of tea-tree, the course falls beautifully across the small site with fairways set amidst the rolling dunes. The more exposed holes atop the ridges offer great views out to Port Philip Bay while the roar of Bass Strait is within earshot on many of the early holes.

A beautifully dipping first fairway is a strong start to the round and one of the prettiest holes on the Peninsula. The 5th and 6th are superb driving holes built across the sloping ridges, with recent tree clearing on the elevated 6th tee and the addition of menacing fairway bunkers down the previously blind left side creating an awesome view of the course's wildest fairway. The wonderful 8th, 11th, 15th and 17th holes also come complete with fabulous fairway undulation, while the driveable 13th, its green perched on the horizon, is the sort of classic short hole that many modern courses struggle to replicate.

The modern golf boom on the Mornington Peninsula has helped rejuvenate Portsea with the increased competition forcing the club, through local designer Michael Clayton, to make subtle improvements to its much-celebrated layout. Encroaching tea-tree was cleared on several holes, while the previously weaker back nine was hardened significantly.

As Clayton explains, 'Portsea's major weakness was the back nine which was made up of short par fours and desperately needed two shot holes that challenged the good player'. He adds that 'the only hole that wasn't a drive and a wedge was the 13th which was driveable'. By lengthening the 15th and 17th and building a new one shot 16th, Clayton has strengthened the softer back nine and added some sting to the Portsea tail.

Measuring less than 6000 metres, the course remarkably manages to test every club in your bag. The reachable par fives and four short par fours ensure plenty of birdie opportunities, although the vagaries of the Peninsula winds and the small greens will keep you on your toes throughout the round.

'Portsea is one of my favourite courses because the land is so dramatic and there are so many shots that are fun to hit and so many holes that are fun to play.'

Michael Clayton

Portsea's 6th fairway with Mother Nature's natural movement and Clayton's sensational bunkering.

The National Golf Club, Ocean Course

Course opened: 2000
Designers: Peter Thomson, Michael Wolveridge, Ross Perrett

'The Ocean Course is as close to a natural old links as anything available outside of Britain.'
Michael Wolveridge

Following the success of its Trent Jones Jr masterpiece, the National Golf Club sought to expand its golfing empire by building two new courses along the stunning coastal sand hills of Cape Schanck. Despite a remote location, the project was a major marketing success thanks to the involvement of Australia's most successful professional golfers, Peter Thomson (Ocean) and Greg Norman (Moonah), who each designed a course on the glorious site.

For the team of Thomson and design partner Michael Wolveridge, the site for their Ocean Course provided a truly splendid assortment of endless sand hills and complemented the pair's philosophies perfectly. Their traditional style of design had seemingly found its ideal canvas.

Wolveridge describes the essential feature of the course as 'its proximity to the sea and extensive views. Most of the time the course meanders through spectacular dune valleys, occasionally rising unexpectedly to capture magnificent views of the Bass Strait'.

The key from the design perspective was to understand the land and find the best fit of holes. Modern advancements in earth moving equipment, that had allowed Trent Jones Jr to create holes on the old course by moving up to a million tons of dirt during its construction, were famously ignored. Instead, the intrepid designers, intent on causing little disruption to the fragile natural landscape, sought to 'find' holes that had fallen naturally across the existing terrain.

In time-honoured traditions, they painstakingly walked the site on foot with tees, turn-points and green sites staked as they presented themselves. For months the designers played around with various combinations of holes, visually playing and walking the course many times whilst the animals grazed in the pasture.

When the time came to finally define the holes, only minor earthworks were needed with Wolveridge and his shaper starting at the first hole and arriving six months later at the 18th.

The stunning view down the 18th and across the Ocean Course, taken at the opening of the National's new clubhouse.

As he explains, this process ensured that the remnant vegetation was not disturbed while fairways 'retained the subtle undulations of the existing landform, thereby revealing their true links character'.

The result is a beautifully wild links layout seamlessly imposed upon the glorious coastal landscape with its wonderful ocean backdrop and fairways that bend through the waving native grasses. The design team preferred to dot the course with their signature pot bunkers and to raise a number of targets to further complicate approach play. The greens are subsequently more exposed to the elements than those next door at Moonah, with holing putts on the slick surfaces awfully difficult in the frequently high winds.

The Ocean experience starts from the very first tee with expansive views over Bass Strait and most of the Peninsula's links land. The par five has a dual fairway split by bunkering, with a more risky high road offering the chance to reach the green in two and the safer low road leaving a much longer approach. The options available here continue throughout the round with sensible course management the key to posting a good score. Most critical is how you play from the tee as the penal pot bunkers cost a full shot when found, yet are easily avoided if tackled conservatively.

Some of the more memorable features of the course are the large sand quarry and beautiful green site at the 4th and the punchbowl 15th green, a throwback to the very finest British links. An interesting aside is the choice of fairway grass, a special Bermuda hybrid, chosen to limit the effect of modern equipment advancements by reducing the run on the sloping fairways. Its thicker cover affords less roll than traditional links grasses yet still retains a smooth and consistent surface.

Along with the adjacent Moonah layout, it's hard to make the case for any Australian course in the past fifty years being built on a more spectacular piece of land. The Ocean Course may not be to everyone's liking, but neither is the Moonah or the Old, and despite inevitable comparisons, the real boon for National members is that all three are wonderfully original and equally compelling.

Moonah Links, Open Course

Course opened: 2001
Designers: Peter Thomson, Michael Wolveridge, Ross Perrett

Australian golf has a new home, the 196-hectare Moonah Links development on Victoria's stunning Mornington Peninsula. Deciding to relocate its entire operations, the Australian Golf Union looked to a farm in remote Rye, more than an hour and a half from its former Melbourne base, to establish the game's new headquarters. While not the first national body to run its operations out of a custom-built golf facility, the Australian version is possibly the most ambitious.

Central to the overall concept is a stadium course purpose-built to regularly host the nation's Open Championship, yet like St Andrews remaining open for public play year round. The responsibility for building the Open Course went to long-time AGU advisers Peter Thomson and Michael Wolveridge, who used the site's enormous natural dunes to create the first links-style stadium course, providing spectators with wonderful vantage points to watch the tournament action.

A close look at the 4th green, typical of the bunkering and greenside shaping found throughout Moonah Links.

The links-like course is set back from the sea a kilometre or so, with plenty of blind and semi-blind shots, menacing cross bunkers, large undulating greens and tight bouncy fairways. Typically evil pot bunkers are scattered throughout the course, often in the middle of fairways and hidden beyond the hills. Wolveridge described the bunkering as 'the key architectural weapon, and we contrived to create a bunker style, which would suitably punish like no other the champion who strayed from his intended path'. He adds that the putting greens were intended to be 'uncomplicated but sloping, requiring sensible thought, there being so many options, in the approach and type of shot required to be played at the flag'.

Built to AGU specifications, the Open Course measures a whopping 6800 metres from the very back and will torture all that dare take on its every inch. The par threes are all mid to long irons, five of the par fours play longer than 400 metres (up to 449!) and three holes stretch over 515 metres. Throw in the strong and constant coastal winds and you have one hell of a thorough examination.

The shortest par four on the course opens proceedings, gently introducing you to the test to follow with the green fittingly nestled among the area's wonderful Moonah trees. Equally as appropriate is the brutal 580 metre par five finishing hole, which into the wind can take three woods to reach and comes complete with a dozen or so pot bunkers scattered throughout the fairway.

The pay for play concept necessitated the building of forward tees for the masses with the distance between the back and social tee boxes more noticeable here than at any other Australian course. Weekend golfers, unable to bribe their way into clubs like Royal Melbourne and The Australian, will be excited by the prospect of tackling an Open course and enjoy saving almost 600 metres by playing from the forward tees. Unfortunately, those caught between are the aficionados and single figure golfers who generally prefer to tackle every metre of a golf course yet are not quite capable of taming a 6800 metre brute in the typically stiff winds. These golfers often find the prospect of playing from social plates most undignified.

Conceptually compelling, the Open Course at Moonah Links has helped define this modern period as the era of the stretched golf course. With its traditional style and modern length, the course provides the ultimate examination of today's rapidly improving golf professional and is among the toughest tests anywhere on the planet.

Looking back down the frightfully difficult closing fairway; its undulation masks a minefield of sand.

The Bellarine Peninsula

Thirteenth Beach Golf Links

Course opened: 2001
Designer: Tony Cashmore

As crazy as it seems now, for fifty years a jam company farmed the Thirteenth Beach site for asparagus. Cattle farmers then took over for a further twenty years before entrepreneur Duncan Andrews restored order to a crazy world by converting this divine land into what it was surely meant for—world-class golf.

Incorporating a three kilometre stretch of stunning surf beach frontage, the Peninsula property is quite extraordinary and moved Tom Watson to declare prior to construction that it was as good a piece of golf land as he'd seen anywhere. Along its ocean boundary, the course stretches deep into rugged sand dune country full of natural dips and ridges and thick coastal vegetation. The same team that built The Dunes on the other side of Melbourne's Port Phillip Bay managed to use these incredible features to create another seaside classic along the Barwon Heads coastline.

The course opens by taking golfers in a loop away from the shore and through low-lying farming pastures before heading in among the sand hills for which the site has become most famous. Designer Tony Cashmore explains that the diversity of these landscapes presented a two-fold design challenge, the first 'to start and finish as many holes within the duneland, and the second to develop the character of the broad farmland so that the entire golfscape would hold together convincingly'.

Within the rolling dunes, holes essentially formed themselves, and for Cashmore the routing became a matter of defining the natural terrain 'to produce par 3, par 4 and par 5 statements as required for a balanced golfing journey'. The flatter land required more work, however, and the designer was able to showcase his skills by building a number of very good holes on vastly inferior land. Many of these inland holes flank the residential development yet are only marginally less impressive than the coastal stretch.

The nature of the landscape and strength of the regional winds ensured a minimalist approach to the design, with little earth moved and the layout thankfully complemented by

The 'driveable but dangerous' 5th, which takes golfers toward the sand dunes for the first time.

generous fairways, large sensible putting surfaces and wild ungroomed bunkering that sits perfectly within its surrounds.

Despite an awesome backdrop and a host of thrilling moments, for me the collection of seaside holes built within the raw dunes are the highlight, particularly the par threes at 7, 12 and 16. Framed by wild sand and surrounded by the song of a pulsating ocean, they are among the most attractive short holes yet discovered in this country. The 16th is the obvious standout hole, and despite playing little more than 100 metres, is one of the most menacing, requiring anything from a soft sand wedge to a piercing six iron. The tiny thumbnail green is set on a spur, semi-concealed by a sandy waste foreground and totally at the mercy of the elements. This setting is a unique mix of the length and contouring of the 10th at Kingston Heath and the sheer rugged beauty of the 7th at The National.

Thirteenth Beach gets its name from the adjacent surf beach, which in turn was named after the famous hole at neighbouring Barwon Heads Golf Club. As a tribute, an eye-catching wasteland bunker was built behind the 6th green, in view of golfers at Barwon Heads and hopefully enticing enough to lure them away for a round. The bunker was added at the insistence of Andrews who also ensured the aggressive line over distant sand traps at the driveable par four 5th measured precisely the same yardage as the famous carry on the 10th at Royal Melbourne West. Although a touch gimmicky, neither 'secret' is apparent and thankfully the Cashmore design is not compromised with both holes among the course's most interesting.

By virtue of the central figures involved and design style used, the course is inevitably compared with the team's earlier work at The Dunes. Thanks largely to the holes within the towering sand hills, Thirteenth Beach wins on individual WOW factor but loses on collective strength and cohesion. As to the question of which will rise highest in popular opinion, it's a split decision dependent upon personal preference and ranking criteria. The only sensible solution for curious golfers, therefore, is to take the ferry across the bay and play both.

Just one of three magnificent short holes, the 12th with its dune setting and rugged bunkering is about as natural as golf gets.

Barwon Heads Golf Club

Course opened: 1921
Designer: Victor East

Founded in 1907, the Barwon Heads Golf Club moved to its present home, alongside the coastal dunes of the Bellarine Peninsula, in 1920. The course was designed by Royal Melbourne professional Victor East and built using horses to plough fairways, tees and greens. With native grasses considered unsuitable, hard-working members followed the ploughs, hand-planting couch grass that had been carted up from Sandringham.

The layout covers two distinct landscapes, the first six holes built on classic windswept links land, while the next twelve play back among the tight coastal tea-tree with the same natural fairway movement but less standout moments. Initially all eighteen were laid out through scrub west of the clubhouse, but when the open links area was leased from the government in the late 1920s, the existing holes were reshuffled to accommodate the new set-up. Incredibly, the course has survived virtually untouched ever since, with the odd hole lengthened but few other changes of any significance.

The most outstanding feature at Barwon Heads remains the exposed opening holes. Built within ear shot of the ocean and adjacent to the seaside sand hills, there is a distinctly understated charm about this part of the course. The 3rd is the pick of these holes with a right bending fairway set across the tee and played over an enormous sandy waste area. Generally heading into the prevailing southwesterly, the temptation is to carry as much of this waste as possible to shorten the approach into an elevated green. The next two tees offer elevated views down the Barwon coast while the 6th continues the links theme with its green bordered by typically British looking rough covered hillocks.

The par three 13th is clearly the back nine's highlight and one of the state's most notorious short holes. Appearing relatively simple, the small drop-kick green is bunkerless, surrounded by wicked undulation and totally exposed to the elements. Though little more than a short iron punch, the beautiful target is always a devil to hit.

Barwon Heads is a prime example of a classic course technology is supposedly rendering obsolete. Tackled with the latest equipment and without the usually stiff coastal breezes, the

The fabulous approach to the par four 9th at Barwon Heads, with a tea-tree covered hillock framing the target.

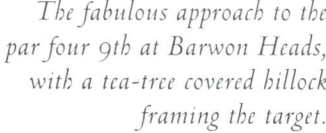

Tiny but treacherous, the famous 13th hole, which the nearby beach was named after.

track seems short, wide and straightforward. However, such conditions are rare for these parts and pitting your skills against this natural golf course and scavenging for pars on seemingly defenceless holes is surprisingly invigorating.

Although not technically a true links, parts of the course offer the most authentic replication of the ancient game found anywhere in Victoria. Like many traditional links, the small greens and pot bunkers lack the refinement and sophistication of modern competitors, with the adjacent Thirteenth Beach providing a stark reminder of how far green shaping has come since the early 1920s.

Steeped in tradition Barwon Heads has famously resisted change over many decades and as a result hasn't kept pace with the modern game quite as successfully as a club like Portsea. Nonetheless, the course remains an exciting and surprisingly relevant test of golfing skills and smarts.

Other Victorian Courses

The Huntingdale Golf Club

Course opened: 1941
Designers: Charles Alison (1941), Jack Newton, Graeme Grant, John Spencer (1998)

One of Australia's most famous tournament venues, Huntingdale was designed by an Englishman, Charles Alison, who never actually set foot on the site. Built on a narrow stretch of former swampland, the routing here is the least interesting of all the Melbourne Sandbelt courses as holes run predominantly north—south and without the tremendous variety found at neighbouring clubs.

As immaculately presented as any Sandbelt course in spring and summer, for many years the members suffered through soggy winters with the continued drainage problems forcing the club to undertake a radical upgrade in the 1990s. The changes, made by Newton, Grant and Spencer, were the most sweeping of any classic course in Victoria and while the year round playability has improved, the upgrade in many ways divided the club.

The biggest disappointment with the new layout is that the best par threes, fours and fives have been diminished and much of the course's character lost forever. The most noticeable loss is the short par three 15th, which had been regarded as one of our finest and most intricate classical one shotters, but was flattened and replaced by a longer, uninspiring resort-style hole.

Huntingdale may never have been the best course on the Sandbelt but it was always a great challenge, and those who played the former course in its Masters-time summer glory will remember it as a truly wonderful experience. There are still enough fine holes to make the course well worth a look but this grand old lady of Australian golf unfortunately 'ain't what she used to be'.

The Heritage Golf and Country Club
Course opened: 2000
Designer: Jack Nicklaus

Nestled among the rolling hills of Melbourne's Yarra Valley, the Heritage Country Club's St John course was the first private Nicklaus course to open in Australia. An interesting mix of parkland and heathland styles, the layout includes several man-made lakes, built primarily to ensure playing surfaces were raised above the river's flood plain.

The best holes at Heritage come around the middle of the round with the most obvious a sweeping par four at the 8th which beautifully follows the sloping ground. The 'signature' Nicklaus holes are the double water carry par five 9th and the par three 11th played across a lake towards a green resting beneath a rock quarry. Nicklaus described the site as an obvious location for the green and it certainly makes for a great picture, but is probably a club too long, especially considering the length of the other par threes.

From the very back tees the course is one of the longest half dozen in the country with the club catering to a range of talents by providing five different tee options. Generally flowing nicely around the attractive site, the course lacks a clever short par four but otherwise provides an excellent and interesting test of your game.

Amstel Golf Club, Ranfurlie Course
Course opened: 2002
Designer: Michael Clayton

Ranfurlie is the second course at the Amstel Golf Club, which was founded back in 1936, and the first full design by Victorian designer Michael Clayton. Located just outside Melbourne's Sandbelt, the course sits on an unattractive yet deceptively undulating property, which proved ideal for golf.

Exposed to the region's high winds, the routing sensibly takes this into account with the long holes running in different directions and the fairways wide enough to provide respite when the wind gets strong, yet strategic enough to test the better players. In order to set up the best angle of approach into the large tilted greens, you often need to nestle the drive close to the fairway traps from the tee. Many of the greens are built on attractive natural rises while the classical bunkering has a wonderfully wild and ungroomed appearance.

Clayton is a man with an unbridled passion for golf within the Sandbelt and his Ranfurlie Course is a reflection of this passion. Most pleasing is that like the very best Melbourne classics, he has also managed to build a number of excellent short par fours and a great set of par threes.

Port Fairy Golf Club

Course opened: 1963
Designers: various

Port Fairy is a charming coastal links built along a series of tumbling sand dunes, with views out to the Southern Ocean and parts of the course almost touching the ocean waters. The club was founded in 1901 but did not move to its present location until 1963. Originally opening with nine holes, the links expanded to a full 18 by 1985 and in 2000 the club employed Michael Clayton to oversee the fine-tuning of this increasingly popular links.

Clayton describes the natural sand hills of Port Fairy as having been 'largely unaltered by man and only mown in order to define fairways and rough'. He adds that the club is developing a higher profile among the golfing community, 'earning the reputation of a golf course worth travelling a long way to play—almost to the point of enjoying cult status'.

The appeal of the Port Fairy Course is apparent from the 15th, a gorgeous coastal par three.

NEW SOUTH WALES AND THE
AUSTRALIAN CAPITAL TERRITORY

Formal golf was introduced to New South Wales in 1882 when the country's first golf club, The Australian, was officially founded at Moore Park in Sydney. The game has grown rapidly since with the state now boasting more golfers and more courses than any other state in Australia.

The greatest concentration of quality courses is naturally found within the greater Sydney area and mostly south of its famous Harbour. Steeped in tradition, the city's big four, pre-Depression clubs—New South Wales, Royal Sydney, The Lakes and The Australian—remain the golfing cornerstones. Unlike the Melbourne boom of the same era where the supply of undulating sandy land was seemingly endless, the development of great golf on great land was hamstrung early in Sydney by rapid population growth. The resultant disparity between the best of Sydney golf and the rest of Sydney golf is quite stark.

Geographically, city golfers remain under-serviced with a continuing call for more courses, particularly within the expanding metropolitan areas. This shortage is in part due to a deficiency in high-quality golf, but also because of the lack of an easily accessible and attractive region for the travelling golfer. The Newcastle/Hunter Valley area is the obvious destination for Sydney golfers, but a little too far from the city to make golf a day trip. The area also lacks the natural attributes of a Mornington Peninsula and is still a handful of really good tracks short of being seriously compared to somewhere like the Gold Coast.

Despite abundant stretches of sandy soil within major centres and scores of popular districts along its well-endowed coastline, the best golf within New South Wales, Sydney aside, is actually scattered far and wide throughout the state. Those prepared to travel for a golf holiday should head south to the Murray River on the state's border with Victoria, which offers low green fees, plenty of sunshine and a series of fine courses free from the usual crowded time sheets. Within the boundaries of the Australian Capital Territory Royal Canberra is the standout, and by quite some margin.

For a single round golf trip outside of Sydney, the most appealing options include the wonderful Newcastle Golf Club north of the city, The Vintage and Horizons courses in the Hunter Valley and the Bonville Resort near Coffs Harbour. This is, of course, assuming that you aren't pals with Kerry Packer and a round at Ellerston is out of the question.

Previous spread: Ellerston Golf Course, 18th hole.

Below: The par three 8th at The Vintage course in the Hunter Valley.

Newcastle Golf Club

Course opened: 1937
Designer: Eric Apperly

Newcastle's 10th green, seemingly innocuous but blind from most sections of an incredible fairway.

Fabulously understated, the Newcastle Golf Club is one of Australian golf's absolute treasures. Originally founded in 1905 near the city of Newcastle, the club built an additional nine hole course on a remote stretch of sand dune country across the harbour at North Stockton in 1915. When a vehicular ferry service finally took golfers directly to Stockton during the 1930s, the site became feasible as the club's home and the permanent move was made. Eric Apperly was commissioned to design a full 18 hole course, which opened in 1937 and has remarkably remained virtually untouched ever since.

Built on beautifully undulating sand hills a short iron from the Hunter River and a few hundred metres from the Pacific Ocean, the course features superb rolling fairways lined by coastal tea-tree and rugged Australian bush that offers a feeling of isolation on virtually every hole. Despite the fertile sandy soil and an obvious deference to the ancient game, this track is uniquely Australian.

In keeping with the finest tradition of courses built during the golden age of golf design, Apperly left the land virtually as he found it and, instead of moving earth, simply cleared the vegetation and routed holes up, over and around the tumbling dunes. The timeless appeal of his design is the wonderful use of this diverse terrain as holes bend and shape with, rather than fight against, the wild fairway movement. Golfers who can accurately attack the hills and ridges here are rewarded with great birdie opportunities while the unsuccessful gamble is usually punished severely.

The small green sites and sandpit-style bunkering lacks the sophistication of the Sandbelt courses built around the same time, but suit the landscape and are intrinsic to the strategy of the design. In fact, when the club recently discovered an old drawing of the original layout and noticed a number of bunkers had gone missing over the years, they had them immediately replaced.

The best collection of holes on the course starts at the incredibly shaped 5th, which is one of the great Australian par fours. A classic driving hole, the fairway is set diagonally across the tee and narrows as it sweeps down and to the left. Surrounded by dense dunes, the risk in taking a driver is that any ball off line is lost in the bush while a solid straight hit generally

funnels down the hill and leaves only a short approach. Those who take the safe option here are left a long and frightening downhill shot from the crest of the fairway towards a tiny target.

The 6th is another gem, with the hole bending left around a steep tea-tree covered hill and its fairway sloping towards trees on the right. The large elevated green is tilted severely from the back and located in a saddle between the dunes. These outstanding holes rank with 14/15 at New South Wales and 17/18 at Royal Melbourne West as the best back-to-back par fours in the country.

Equally attractive, the 7th is Newcastle's most celebrated hole and regarded by some judges as one of the finest par threes in the world. Although not as well known, the short 8th is another classic and built across subtle slopes that rise and fall away towards the outside of the fairway.

On the back nine the standout is the long Roller Coaster 10th, which features three huge dips from tee to green and wins the funkiest fairway in Australia award. Falling away to bush on both sides, each shot is blind or semi-blind depending on your length, and with the green hidden behind the final hill, the approach is exhilarating regardless of whether you attack the ridges or lay-up in the valleys.

Other highlights on the run home include the brilliant tumbling short par four 11th and excellent driving holes at the 14th and 15th. Strengthened with the addition of a new championship tee, pushed some 40 metres back from thick scrub, the 18th is now a terrific hole and a wonderful finish to the round. Though the front nine is more memorable, there is hardly a mediocre moment anywhere on this course.

Highly original and highly rated yet continually under appreciated, the charming Newcastle Golf Club is not just one of the best courses in New South Wales, but one of the finest classics anywhere in Australia.

The Royal Sydney Golf Club

Course opened: 1909
Designer: various

From an original base of twenty members in 1893, the Royal Sydney Golf Club has developed into one of the largest sporting clubs in the world with its influential membership now totalling almost 6000. Despite humble beginnings inland near the present Concord Golf Club, the club's founders were determined to develop a seaside golf links and moved almost immediately to a new home in the Bondi sandhills with a plan to extend its nine hole course east towards the ocean. Sandhill encroachment, however, forced the club to instead gradually shuffle west across Old South Head Road, until the present site was acquired in 1909 and a new 18 hole course developed.

Royal Sydney's glorious clubhouse in full view from its famous finishing hole.

A product of slow meticulous evolution, the golf course is devoid of the signature of any marquee designer and has instead matured through almost 100 years of sensible club management. Located on one of the most expensive pieces of real estate in the country, the billion dollar Rose Bay property is perfectly positioned being only a block from Sydney Harbour and a kilometre from the Pacific Ocean. The terrain is accordingly ideal for a links with the eastern side of the property elevated and tilted towards the centre of the course which, although narrow and much flatter, does not lack minor and interesting undulation. Two thirds of the course runs north–south through this middle section, yet pleasingly these holes are among Royal Sydney's best.

The character of the golf course has developed from a classic links through periods of parkland reform to the unique mix of both styles that members presently enjoy. During the 1960s, the club planted substantial amounts of trees and the feeling by the late 70s was that the original links charm of Royal Sydney had been lost. As the cycle continued, a large number of trees was then removed, with the stunning final hole a vivid example of how the two styles

Heavily bunkered down the right but best approached from the left, the 8th is nonetheless Royal Sydney's best short par four.

were intertwined. The tee shot is played through a chute of mature gums to a dogleg where the trees end and a large open rolling green, framed by the magnificent clubhouse, is presented.

The front nine covers the more interesting terrain and opens with a clever short par four played from the shadows of the clubhouse and recently reshaped to incorporate a slight dogleg. The more difficult inward nine starts with back-to-back long par fours before moving to the tight mid-length 12th with thick trees that narrow significantly the further you drive, and a wonderful double green, built during the 1980s. The finish to the round is particularly strong, with a beautifully bunkered long hole, a tough par three and the brilliant 18th forming a superb closing stretch.

Originally the epitome of penal design, there were at one stage as many as 350 bunkers dotted throughout the course, mostly lining the sides of fairways. In 1926, Dr Alister MacKenzie recommended that to make the test more strategic, as many as three-quarters could be removed, describing the traps as being of little interest to golfers and 'actually creating bad players owing to their cramping effect'. Despite a steep fee and high reputation, his recommendations were not implemented at the time, although gradually many of the bunkers that irked MacKenzie were removed.

In the late 1970s, with the course in dire need of an upgrade, Peter Thomson and Michael Wolveridge were commissioned to improve greenside bunkering and reshape the greens with most built up to fall away into steep, closely mown hollows. By 2002, the club again felt the greens needed improvement and employed Ross Watson to reconstruct and slightly recontour all eighteen using a new fine leaf creeping bentgrass it hoped would achieve a firmness, texture and speed similar to that experienced on Melbourne's Sandbelt. As a consequence of firmer putting surfaces, the bunker styling also needed attention, and happily the larger classical bunkers that previously existed on holes 2 and 16, as remnants of a past era, became the model for the new work. Some additional bunkers were needed while existing traps were either rebuilt or reshaped to achieve a consistent style throughout.

Watson explains that 'from an initial plan to replace the putting surfaces evolved a total facelift, the objective being to return the course to something like its former windswept rustic links feel as opposed to the parkland feel which had gradually taken over from the mid-1960s'.

Shifting from a penal to strategic design and from seaside to parkland and back again in appearance, Royal Sydney now strikes the perfect balance between a strong challenge to the better players and providing what MacKenzie refers to as 'pleasurable excitement' to its members and guests.

Royal Canberra Golf Club

Course opened: 1962
Designers: John Harris, James Scott

Golf courses are generally developed without great assistance from local governments, as designers often have to endure tremendous battles with bureaucrats to ensure their designs are approved. In the Australian Capital Territory, however, the Royal Canberra Golf Club exists as the region's golfing gem thanks largely to the hand of local government in condemning its original home and selecting a new and remarkable replacement.

The club's current Westbourne Woods site was initially set up as an arboretum for botanists to plant and plan the trees used throughout the city of Canberra. The first plantings were made in 1915 and included Californian and Mediterranean pines, blue-grey cyprus from Arizona, birch from English forest glades and cedars from the Himalayas, as well as countless natives.

Looking back down Royal Canberra's par five finishing hole.

In the 1940s, with the city developed and the Woods surplus to requirements, it was suggested that the government build a golf course on the site and seek a club to manage and preserve the area. Around the same time, the government also decided that it needed to flood parts of the city's major lakes to enhance and preserve its water supply. The original home of Royal Canberra, on the Molonglo River bank, was earmarked as land to be submerged.

The Department of the Interior engaged architect James Scott to advise on the layout of the new Westbourne Woods course while it searched for appropriate site custodians. Scott's plan sensibly took full advantage of the natural topography and the many established species within the arboretum. Fairways were shaped and some additional plantings made, yet the partly constructed course sat dormant for years while politicians debated the finer details of the lakes scheme, and made arrangements for a club to complete the course and finance the water reticulation.

In 1956, the Senate finally passed the full lakes scheme which sealed the fate of the old Royal Canberra course and assured water storage and supply to Westbourne Woods. With

Royal Canberra agreeing to terms for use of the site, it signalled the start of a great era for golf in the capital.

The club entrusted English architect Commander John Harris to complete the design of the partially built course. Unable to remove many protected trees, he was forced to use Scott's basic routing and to incorporate his own tees, bunkers and greens into the cleared land. The course the two men built is a searching test from the tee, with tight tree-lined fairways that bend in both directions and demand precise shot-making to keep the ball in play. The putting surfaces are generally superb and among the largest in the country, with Harris deciding to build tiers into most of the elevated greens to give players a better look at the flagsticks.

Aside from superb driving holes at the 9th and 10th, the 16th is the highlight and one of those rare holes worth travelling vast distances to play. The fairway is encased by magnificent Monterey pines, and meanders over a stunning rise and enormous dip before climbing towards its huge elevated green. Long hitters can today bomb drives over the hill and be left only a short iron, but the ryegrass fairways offer less roll than traditional couch and these longer drives usually pull up on the downslope leaving a tricky uphill approach from a hanging lie. Uniquely Royal Canberra, this is one of Australia's truly great golf holes.

Due to the diversity of the plant life, some corners of the course are less dramatic than holes like the 16th, but there are more than enough quality moments throughout the round to compensate for any character changes. Since opening in 1962, the only significant course alterations were made during the 1980s when holes 4 through 6 were redesigned by Peter Thomson and Michael Wolveridge, who also returned years later to design the clubs third loop of nine holes.

In horticultural terms, the Royal Canberra site is one of the most significant in world golf with more than 220 species of trees and plants found throughout the course. In golfing terms, however, it's the wonderful design as much as the natural beauty of the Westbourne Woods that makes Royal Canberra one of our very finest courses, and for this fabulous bounty we should all thank Canberra's politicians.

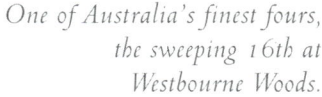

One of Australia's finest fours, the sweeping 16th at Westbourne Woods.

The Lakes Golf Club

Course opened: 1928
Designers: Robert Von Hagge, Bruce Devlin (1970)

The Lakes Golf Club was born in 1928 when a barren waste of sandhills surrounding Sydney's largest wetland water body was leased to a group of keen golfers for the purpose of building its links. The club was forced to share this water system with an adjacent public course by a council who clearly did not see the incredible potential of a composite course around the main lakes.

Today The Lakes is one of Australia's most distinguished golf clubs, thanks largely to an association with professional golf that dates back to the 1930s and its original course, designed by Eric Apperly, which was destroyed in 1968 when the government reclaimed part of the site to build a freeway.

Part of a series of famous closing par fives, the 14th is an exciting hole though it lacks the lay-up options of the 11th.

With the demise of their beloved course came a period of considerable hardship as members were encouraged to golf elsewhere while the road was constructed and the golf course rebuilt. As reconstruction neared completion, the club was shocked to discover that many former members had established close ties with new clubs and were reluctant to return. In desperation, 70 life memberships were offered for a one-off fee of $3000, and it was the support from these members that eventually secured the club's finances and ensured its short-term survival.

The Lakes that greeted members on opening day in 1970 was vastly different from the one they had departed just two years earlier. None of the original 18 holes was retained and the clubhouse had been relocated from its position behind the current 14th tee to a more central location, allowing both loops of nine to return to the same point. With the freeway dissecting the site, two distinct nines were created, one built almost entirely around the wetlands and the other on less spectacular land to the west. Although the 'dry' land had enough natural sandy undulation to expedite some fine holes, it is unquestionably the wonderful back nine water moments that steal the show.

The front nine starts with a tantalising par four alongside the lake that introduces the water theme and acts as a teaser for the fun to follow. Golfers then head under the freeway to the parkland holes before returning to the main site at the short 9th.

Following the intriguing 10th, the course moves onto its signature hole, a long and exceptionally strategic par five bending around the main lake. Though most play safely down the fairway and pitch across the water, the longer hitters hoping to reach this peninsula green in two must drive as close to the water as possible to set up the thrilling all-carry approach. The back nine par fives are the highlight with the 14th and 17th also playing around the lakes, and reachable for the brave who can take on the water.

Another outstanding hole is the 16th, which takes full advantage of the natural water systems running through the site. Lakes and bunkers narrow the fairway and force most to back off their driver, yet the further back from the tee the more water you must carry on the approach. Legendary golf writer Tom Ramsey once described this as Sydney's finest par four.

Along with The Australian, The Lakes Mk II is the most celebrated Australian course built between the Great Depression and the present era. While Nicklaus worked along existing lines but demolished the original character of The Australian, here Von Hagge and Devlin invented eighteen totally new holes, yet managed to retain the characteristics that had made The Lakes so popular.

The Lakes best and most recognisable hole, the long par five 11th.

With a bounty of thrills and challenges, the finale to each nine is almost anti-climactic, with straightforward par threes played away from the lakes and towards the huge clubhouse. While there is no questioning the collective strength of the holes, it seems a shame that the old clubhouse site could not be retained or a more spectacular alternative selected. Although a very fine golf course, had the routing been able to bring one of the classic closing holes, like the 11th or 17th, back to the clubhouse, or had full access to the wetlands been granted in the early days, The Lakes would have been truly stupendous.

The Australian Golf Club

Course opened: 1904
Designer: Jack Nicklaus (1977)

Though the game of golf had been enjoyed in Australia from as early as 1834, it wasn't until 1882 that golf clubs were formally embraced, the first appropriately named The Australian. Steeped in prestige, the club was founded at Centennial Park, making its permanent home the current Kensington site in early 1904.

The move not only signalled the birth of a great golf club, but also the nation's Open Championship which the Australian Golf Union decided would be hosted at the new Kensington links. The choice of venue for this inaugural event was strange considering The Australian course hadn't been built and Royal Melbourne, Royal Sydney and Royal Adelaide were the constituent clubs who formed the first AGU council. Unfortunately, little is known of the politics behind the decision.

Typical of the long par fours at The Australian, the 17th green is small, fast, protected by a pond and angled across the fairway.

During the 1960s, The Australian lost part of its site when the New South Wales government reclaimed land to expand Sydney's freeways. With layout changes enforced upon the club, a move towards an American style of design was resisted and Victorian Sloan Morpeth instead employed as course consultant. The resistance to American-style would not last long, however, as a few years later the links fell victim to the most radical course upgrade in Australian history.

Kerry Packer's Consolidated Press had taken over the running of the Australian Open in 1975, conceiving the idea to fully commercialise and televise the event with Packer's home club, The Australian, as the venue. Stunning the golf world by producing the first tee to green coverage of all 18 holes, he then dropped a bombshell by informing the club that he wanted Jack Nicklaus to totally redesign the golf course in time for the 1977 Open.

The imposing opening tee shot on the double dogleg par five 1st hole.

Tougher and custom-built to host the event, the course would be set up for television and feature smaller greens and increased mounding and hazards with the full costs of the redesign at Mr Packer's expense. Despite strong objection, his proposal was narrowly passed and the classic links transformed into an American parkland course. Nicklaus made further changes after the first Open, then returned the following year to capture his sixth and final title on the course he'd built. The layout has seen very little change since.

While alterations to the Morpeth routing were very minor, the playing characteristics were totally abolished. The blind shots were removed, natural sandhills converted to rough covered mounds, and the generous fairways were narrowed and defined by a dense second cut. To the horror of traditionalists, their beloved links was transposed with tall trees, thick rough, small subtle greens and the bane of all traditional golf courses—water hazards.

The firm, fast greens are guarded by sculptured undulations, deep unforgiving sand traps and small ponds, with most slightly offset against the fairways to place extreme pressure on the long game. Unusually, the longer holes are actually protected by the smallest and most severe greens, and particularly punishing on the overzealous.

Each nine concludes with a series of adjacent long holes running back and forth to maximise the effect of seasonal winds. The 7th through 9th is a brutal stretch with three long narrow two-shotters played to small greens guarded by ponds and fearsome bunkers. The final holes on the back nine are only marginally tamer, with the 16th and 17th long par fours typically severe on the missed shot and the 18th a classic mid-length par five complete with a lake to catch those who press too hard for a closing birdie.

Rating The Australian is a difficult assignment because each golfer takes something different away from their experience here. Personally, I find the course a grind, tough and unforgiving, but also unusually compelling for such an unspectacular site. The long holes are the standouts, but its unrelenting pressure gets to you more than its length as there are no obvious birdie opportunities and no breathers.

The Vintage Golf Club

Course opened: 2003
Designers: Greg Norman, Bob Harrison

The Hunter Valley, two hours north of Sydney, is a Mecca for food and wine enthusiasts from all over the country, catering in particular to the discerning Sydney market. Thanks to The Vintage development, Australia's most popular wine-growing district now also caters to a sophisticated golf market looking to acquire exclusive golf course real estate in the heart of this fashionable locale.

Surrounded by picturesque vineyards, historical wineries and rolling hills, this charming site was far from the ideal base with which to build a championship golf course, due to the diversity of its topography. Rather than fight the contrasting landscapes by manufacturing holes, the designers instead opted to allow the lie of the land, as much as the development master plan, to dictate the flow and style of the golf course. The result therefore is that The Vintage is far from your typical signature design.

Starting off within the open bushland, the course soon winds its way around undisturbed creeks and gullies, through small areas of forest and even alongside the local vineyards. The outward nine tends to play more through the undulating wilderness, while the back nine features less fairway movement but incorporates more of the naturally occurring wetlands. Though the collective strength of the front side is possibly greater, it's the wonderfully original holes on the run home that are certain to capture most golfers' imagination.

Several fine driving holes start the round, including the attractive 2nd which bends hard right through a chute of casuarinas and over a small creek towards a deliciously bunkered narrow green. The short par four 4th is another classic driving hole, as is the strong 6th with its large green, partially hidden beyond ridges of wild kangaroo grass. Most of the natural wooded landscape occurs within these first six holes, and the design emphasis was on dropping holes into the site without touching more of the bushland than absolutely necessary. As a result, fairways are quite narrow, especially when compared with the wide playing areas throughout the rest of the course.

The strategy of the more open back nine hinges largely on a number of existing ponds, creeks and gullies. The fun starts at the incredible 10th, a lengthy par five that swings down towards a lake and large ridge, with its unique green perched six metres atop a clay-faced cliff and featuring a wild grassy mound that eats into the putting surface.

The attractive par three 5th hole set within rugged bush and played over natural wetlands.

Distant mountains, surrounding vineyards and classical bunkering feature prominently as you approach the par five 7th green.

The 11th highlights the rural charm of the site, with an elevated tee above a dam wall and a flat fairway set across a natural wasteland. A small creek down the right appears insignificant, yet retains an ability to coerce players away which leaves a longer approach back towards the creek and over an enormous ridge obscuring the view of the green.

While it must have been tempting for the designers to reduce the effect of these quirky natural features, their inclusion makes the experience wonderfully unconventional. More conventional is the classical bunkering that surrounds many greens but is used sparingly on the fairways. Many of the better driving holes are actually free of sand and instead use the shape of the land and the site's raw hazards to dictate the strategy.

The Vintage is a course that residents, with the opportunity to uncover its every idiosyncrasy, will particularly enjoy. On just the one sighting, however, the charm is not lost, with my first visit to the course coming months before it opened and leaving a lasting impression. Often the compromise needed to squeeze a golf course within a residential development can lead to disappointing results, but here the course achieves the rare feat of successfully combining a spectacular and challenging design within its residential community. In fact, The Vintage rates with Thirteenth Beach and Brookwater as the most interesting golf/real estate developments in the country and, further to that accolade, is among the top two or three modern courses in New South Wales.

There are certainly more coherent courses, but The Vintage has a rugged unpredictability that few courses will ever match. Despite its young 'vintage', this track is certain to ripen, age well and mature into one of New South Wales' leading golf courses.

Terrey Hills Golf and Country Club
Course opened: 1994
Designers: Graham Marsh, Ross Watson

Built on the fringes of Sydney's Ku-ring-gai Chase National Park, the Terrey Hills Golf and Country Club, which opened in 1994, was the first golf course to be built in Sydney for more than two decades. The success of the course as a professional tournament venue during the 1990s led to a number of new developments around the city's outskirts, yet Terrey Hills remains the best example of modern design in a city where the game is dominated by its celebrated classics.

What sets this course apart from its contemporaries is the wonderfully isolated site, with holes beautifully sculptured from the surrounding forest and meandering through the bush landscape and around a series of integrated water hazards. The front nine has the more

interesting landscape, although the best holes are probably found on the more open and spreadout back nine. Starting the run home is the tough 10th, which bends gently around a lake with a distinctive rolling fairway full of humps and hollows running all the way to the green.

Another fine hole is the long 17th, played from the far corner of the property and alongside Duffy's Forest. A slight kink in the fairway tightens the landing area for the long hitters, while the fairway traps, which actually mark the ideal driving line, tend to force many left into the thick rough. The target here is narrow and the approach fraught with danger as the shot must flirt with a precarious pond that eats into the right side of the green.

Of the front nine holes, the downhill 3rd is a terrific mid-length par four played from within bush and through rows of trees that clear at the landing area. The hole then falls away to set up a thrilling second shot over the edge of a lake to a slender green surrounded by extreme undulation.

In truth, there are actually very few standout moments at Terrey Hills; instead there's a solid collection of eighteen high-quality golf holes set within an attractive and tranquil locale. The course is similar in style to others built by this design team, especially the symmetrical mounding along the sides of the rolling mogul fairways. The national park setting, however, clearly distinguishes it from other Marsh/Watson designs.

An excellent championship layout, Terrey Hills probably works even better as a course where the average player can enjoy a challenging round of golf and still manage to post a decent score. The playing surfaces are always fabulous, with fairway widths kept generous for the weak hitter but narrowing significantly where the professionals drive. The large greens are also superb and similarly playable to golfers of any ability. Often narrow at the front, they come complete with tiers, swales and plenty of interesting breaking putts.

Unlike many modern courses, which attempt to tame the best by torturing the rest, Terrey Hills is a challenge that golfers of all standards are sure to enjoy.

Concord Golf Club

Course opened: 1916
Designers: Dan Soutar, Ross Watson

One of Sydney's leading tournament venues, the Concord Golf Club's origins can be traced back to 1893 when the nine hole Sydney Golf Club was founded at Concord West. By the end of the year, the club had acquired additional land in the Bondi sandhills and in 1899 relinquished the Concord site to local members to form their own club.

A few short years later, fearing their course would be sold for residential development, the members merged with the Strathfield Golf Club and opened an 18 hole men's and 9 hole ladies course on nearby land. With the purchase of an adjacent site in 1916, the ladies course was closed and a complete remodel of the old course undertaken by Dan Soutar.

For more than 80 years, members then enjoyed their course virtually unchanged, but in the late 1990s, with modern technology strangling the challenge and the club preparing to host professional tournaments, a significant facelift was required. The small acreage made radical change impossible so the club instead decided to tweak rather than tear the course apart.

Designer Ross Watson was employed to reshape bunkers, landing areas and many tee complexes in an attempt to strengthen the test. He also rebuilt all eighteen greens and replaced the grass with a Penncross A4 bentgrass, which is possibly the world's quickest putting surface.

Watson describes the club's intention in upgrading the course as being 'in order keep pace with advancements in the game and to retain its reputation as a genuine tournament venue'. He adds that 'the course was previously known for its smallish elevated greens and steep banks, and from a design point of view, the main challenge was to increase the size yet retain the challenge of small greens. This was achieved by designing greens with slightly oblique "wings" where pins could be placed and defended by greenside bunkers, slopes and swales'. The Watson changes were not only well received but also helped Concord climb back up various rankings lists.

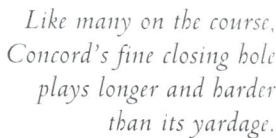

Like many on the course, Concord's fine closing hole plays longer and harder than its yardage.

The course remains beautifully treed, with undulating fairways winding up and over gentle rises and bending around a collection of established trees. The anti-clockwise routing includes the unusual combination of back-to-back par threes at the 9th and 10th, and a number of attractive mid to long par fours that fall nicely across the natural terrain.

Not an overly long course, the great challenge at Concord is keeping the ball in play and managing your short game around the tiny treacherous greens. Driving is generally tight, as the intruding trees and heavy fairway bunkering tends to narrow the fairways significantly. The key to scoring well, however, remains a good short game, with chipping and pitching from the thick kikuyu fairways and fringes to the small fast greens particularly difficult. In fact, from inside 50 metres, Concord may well be the toughest test in the whole country.

Bonville International Golf Resort

Course opened: 1992
Designers: Terry Watson, Ted Stirling

Along with Laguna Quays and Joondalup, the beautiful Bonville resort on the New South Wales north coast is probably the ideal resort for those wishing to take the non-golf partner on their next golf holiday. The beauty of the area is breathtaking, and with plenty to distract those averse to our great game, you are usually able to enjoy your golf free from any hint of petulance.

The overwhelming attractiveness of Bonville strikes the moment you drive through the gates, with the resort and enchanting golf course literally carved through an undulating forest of huge flooded gums and native rainforest. Perfect for weddings, romantic getaways and relaxing sabbaticals, the beauty of the resort almost distracts from the fact that this is also a very fine golf course.

Featuring one of the most dramatic sites in Australian golf, the steep elevation change from tee through green provides plenty of stunning views over and across the sloping ground with each hole totally secluded and surrounded by gums and dense forest foliage. Keeping the ball in play from the tee is an absolute imperative, while hitting greens in regulation is the biggest challenge because judging approach shots into the small targets from fairway crests and depressions can be awfully difficult.

There are a number of fine moments throughout the round including numerous water holes and roller coaster fairways on the 2nd, 5th and 18th. The approach into the 2nd green from the summit of the fairway over an enormous gully is especially memorable. The short dogleg 16th hole, with a creek dissecting the fairway and a small pond fronting the green, is another highlight, as is the rarely played 17b emergency par three over a gorgeous lily-filled pond, and which is only used when other holes are out of action.

Bonville's immaculate garden beds and surrounding grounds, complete with scores of flowering plants including azaleas, have at various times had owners trumpeting the course as Australia's Augusta. While some real estate similarities do exist, the golf course is nothing like the MacKenzie masterpiece and is best judged on its own style and individuality.

It's the awesome setting and wonderful serenity that sets Bonville apart and makes the course a favourite among travelling golfers. So popular is it, in fact, that if there were a people's choice award for Australian courses, my guess is that Bonville would probably challenge Royal Melbourne for top honours. Few could argue that its architecture gets anywhere near the classic courses, yet there is an undeniable charm here that few modern tracks can match and that resort golfers love.

Bonville's gorgeous 'spare' hole, 17b, with its green framed by an enchanting forest of flooded gums.

Since opening back in 1992, the condition of the course has continued to improve as the maintenance team have learnt to better manage the problems associated with its forest setting and lack of direct sunlight. My advice, therefore, to anyone who has not seen the course since its early days, is to return with speed, while those who have never been before should seriously consider treating themselves to the country's most resplendent resort golf experience.

Camden Lakeside Country Club

Course opened: 1993
Designers: Peter Thomson, Michael Wolveridge, Ross Perrett

When the multinational company that owns the famous Old Course Hotel sought to extend its global golfing empire into Australia, they turned to rugged farmland outside of Sydney and the same designers who had previously built their successful 'Dukes course' at St Andrews.

Although Camden Lakeside is worlds away from the famous ancient links of Scotland, the course pays homage to their legacy through a typically traditional design. The greens are generous and straightforward and the fairways full of clever undulation and fiendish pot bunkers built to punish the stray or over aggressive. As designer Peter Thomson explains, 'the real challenge at Camden Lakeside is getting to the green. Once there, putting should be fun on generally flat surfaces, just as you would find on classic old courses'.

The opening hole highlights this philosophy, as the seemingly simple approach must avoid a deep creek and cunning hollows that push balls towards the two small traps that guard the large green. The adjacent 4th green is tucked into the side of a hill and also positioned beyond the creek, with these same subtle twists and turns around its fringe. For those daring enough to play the hole from the tips, it also features a 220 metre water-carry off the tee.

One of the more interesting holes is the par five 5th, with any ball heading right off its elevated tee ending out of bounds among cows from an adjoining property. The second shot is fairly simple but must avoid visually misleading bunkers that appear closer than they actually are due to the seemingly natural fairway bumps. Perception is often your greatest adversary at Camden Lakeside.

Sunrise over the first fairway at Camden Lakeside.

Despite a number of other fine holes, the highlight at Camden comes at the death with two closing holes as strong as any in Sydney. Pushing 430 metres, the 17th is the longest par four on the course and comes complete with a semi-blind uphill approach played through a copse of banksias towards an enormous target. Par here is richly satisfying but easily undone on the very next hole.

The 18th is a grandstand finish, more contemporary than classic, with water left and a tight fairway titled diagonally across the tee. A huge lone gum stands in the middle of the landing area forcing the golfer to either play the hole straight and over the lake or as a dogleg by hitting right of the tree and leaving a longer approach. The brave line must not only carry the lake but also split the tree and a row of pot bunkers along the water's edge.

While long holes with heroic water carries are hardly traditional, the combination of classical style bumps and bunkering and contemporary hazards with risk/reward alternatives are successfully integrated into this natural Australian landscape. Built for the owners of St Andrews' most famous hotel, by the Old Course's most fervent devotees, Camden Lakeside is yet another fascinating reminder of one golf course's extraordinary power to influence the work of men half a world away.

Horizons Golf Resort
Course opened: 1992
Designers: Graham Marsh, Ross Watson

Located on the New South Wales mid-north coast, the Horizons Golf Resort is situated within a rugged area of tea-tree laden swamp only minutes from the popular seaside town of Port Stephens.

The golf course site takes in a series of topography changes with holes shaped through tall eucalypts, around natural wetlands, melaleuca swamps and pristine man-made lakes. The contrasting waterways are the most significant feature of the land with the designer's intent to incorporate these natural features as much as possible into the routing.

Holes not built around the water hazards instead weave through the Australian bush and are among the most enjoyable on the course, particularly towards the end of the round. Aside from the 10th and 18th, the back nine is beautifully set in a secluded and picturesque forest of tall natives and tea-tree, while the front nine loops around the wetlands and two major lakes.

Short but tight, the tricky par three 8th hole.

Course designer Ross Watson describes the experience of golf at Horizons as 'full of surprises with most holes separate and well-camouflaged from the others by the remnant tea-tree'. He adds that the holes are 'individual by design and therefore very memorable, but the overlying memory is the need to be in control of one's game due to the nature and proximity of the tea-tree and the ocean breezes which cool the course daily'.

One of the fine holes at Horizons is the 8th, a delightfully indigenous short hole measuring just 153 metres. Thick marshland surrounds the green and runs along the right side of the hole while head-high weedy waste lies between tee and green. Short, therefore, is not an option, and three menacing pot bunkers to the left of the green wait to catch those playing too far away from the marsh.

The back nine begins with an excellent long par four played over water to a peninsula fairway bending left around the course's main lake. The drive played close to the water will leave a fairly straightforward approach into a long green, which abuts the 16th green. The view back down the 16th hole from this fairway in fading light is quite stunning.

In true resort style, the final hole runs alongside a voracious water hazard that eats into the right side of the green. Measuring a little over 300 metres and with resort guests and fellow golfers enjoying views out over the green, the potential for great theatre at this concluding hole is evident from the tee. Despite the presence of water, the attacking option is extremely enticing as an aggressive and straight drive sets up a realistic birdie chance.

In many regards, this finale reflects the very nature of the Horizons course itself. A genuine test of your game, the hazards are conspicuous and the best plan of attack apparent, making the challenge fair to golfers of all abilities. Most refreshingly, the course does not go to great pains to ensure that the battle for each birdie is to the death.

Typical of resort golf, Horizons finishes with a water hole, this one throwing up plenty of birdies to those who can stay 'dry'.

Forster–Tuncurry Golf Club, Great Lakes Tuncurry Course

Course opened: 1985
Designers: Kel Nagle, Mike Cooper

While this book celebrates the high profile courses of the present modern era and the celebrated masterpieces of the MacKenzie period, it also unearths a handful of hidden gems which don't sit comfortably within either category. Great Lakes Tuncurry is one such course.

Before building up this secluded treasure too much, I should qualify the review by warning pampered golfers not to expect the same level of service and conditioning experienced at other courses featured in these pages. The minimal green fee you pay reflects the overall standard of grooming, but the lack of lavish trimmings detracts little from the overall experience and is actually part of the charm. This is good old-fashioned golf and for replenishment of the spirit, Tuncurry comes highly recommended.

Situated only a few hundred metres from the ocean, the roar of crashing waves rings in your ears throughout the round despite the thick tea-tree covered sand dunes preventing any water glimpse. The course makes great use of its rugged topography with holes weaving through valleys of sand, surrounded by scrub as they bend naturally around the foliage.

Similar in style to Newcastle, the design lacks Newcastle's sophistication with just a handful of modest bunkers and small straightforward greens. Driving though can be exhilarating, especially downwind, where ever-present risk/reward options allow the aggressive player to attack the doglegs by driving semi-blind over waste areas. Successful tee shots set up great birdie chances while stray balls are lost forever to the region's snakes.

Subject to high coastal winds, the course can be a killer in extreme conditions, but for the unassuming golfer Tuncurry is a wonderful surprise. Fun, tough and interesting, if you enjoy your golf 'raw' then the Great Lakes is definitely for you.

Below and opposite page: Two views of the famous 'Hogan's Hole' at Narooma, one looking across the cliff from the tee and the other across the green and down the coastline.

Narooma Golf Club

Course opened: front nine 1930, back nine 1980
Designer: various (front nine), John Spencer (back nine)

The Narooma Golf Club was immortalised during the 1980s when Paul Hogan filmed one of his 'G'day Mate' Australian commercials from the 3rd green, sitting on clifftops high above the Pacific Ocean. Along the entire New South Wales south coast, this hole remains the standout and one of the most intimidating in the state, with its tiny target perched near the cliff's edge and at least 30 metres above the swirling surf.

The remaining holes are less exciting, although several others on the front nine do use the sloping terrain to offer sweeping views of the ocean and wonderful Glasshouse Rocks. Remarkably, the 5th hole has a burial site, marked with three white crosses, laying only metres from the edge of its green and close to the cliff. Little is known of how the deceased came to be buried within the golf course, but Narooma rumour suggests the graves belong to aviation pioneers who crashed on the site when flying from nearby Montague Island. Who knows? Perhaps they lost one ball too many to 'Hogan's Hole'.

The inland back nine was not built until 1980 and is much less dramatic, with holes carved out of the natural bush and winding around a large lake. The course may not be Australia's best, but Narooma's third hole remains one of our most cherished.

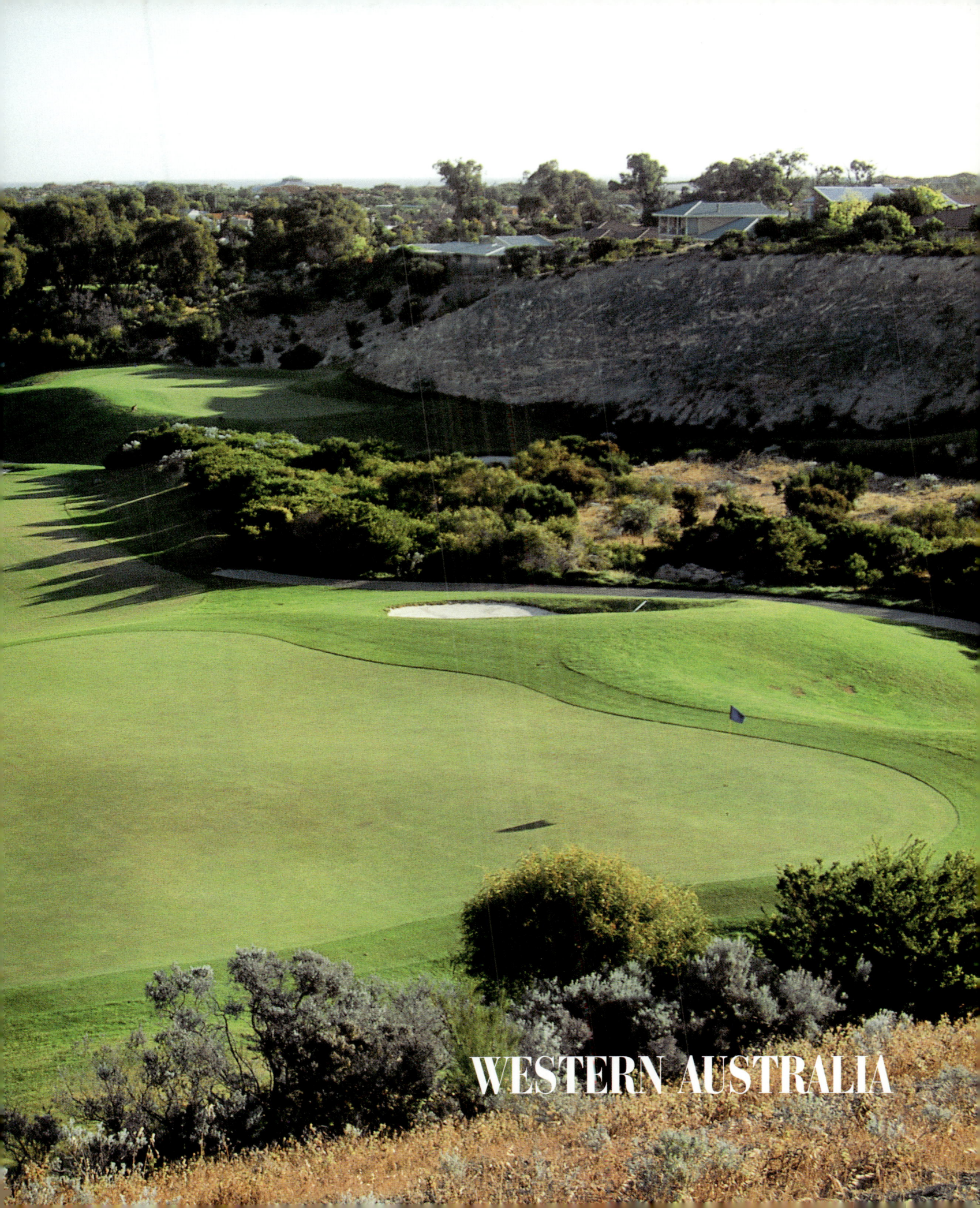

WESTERN AUSTRALIA

Despite its vast size, Western Australia has the least number of golfers and golf courses of any mainland state. Most of the quality courses are concentrated in the south-western corner around Perth and the nearby Peel region, which is less than an hour away and commonly referred to as the Golf Coast. This is a fantastic part of the world for golf with its plentiful supply of sand and mild climate conducive to growing the finest bent and couch grasses and helping to build natural courses with excellent year-round drainage.

The state is enjoying a renaissance of sorts with the much-publicised arrival of Joondalup in 1985 signalling the start of a new golden era of design. Lake Karrinyup had previously existed for decades unchallenged as the region's finest track, and though still the leading championship venue, its ranking has been under constant threat from a string of improving newcomers. The best of these is the newest which looks the oldest, the links at Kennedy Bay.

The most striking aspect of golf within Western Australia is the tremendous variety available with a little bit of everything but not a lot of anything. For private golfers, the classical Sandbelt-style architecture at Karrinyup and Mt Lawley are the highlights, and though different, both supply proud memberships with superb golf in sumptuous surrounds. For the resort or public player, an impressive range of options include The Vines, an archetypal Australian resort course, Meadow Springs with its contrasting landscapes and design, and Joondalup, which is … well, Joondalup and alone would make any region seem diverse.

For something totally different, the fabulous Kennedy Bay offers a traditional links experience, while a suburb away at Secret Harbour lies a raw dune course built among towering sandhills. The oldest course in the state is the often overlooked seaside Albany Golf Club a few hours south-east of Perth, which opened on its current site back in 1899 and retains an old-world charm.

For an economy that can only sustain a small and balanced number of high-end resort courses and member-only private clubs, the overall quality of the golf in and around Perth is outstanding. The courses featured in this book are an incredible assortment of styles and experiences and come highly recommended.

Previous spread: Joondalup Golf Resort, Dune Course 3rd hole.

Right: The par four 2nd hole at Kennedy Bay south of Perth.

Lake Karrinyup Country Club

Course opened: 1928
Designer: Alex Russell

As the only mainland state that Dr MacKenzie did not visit during his whirlwind 1926 tour, Western Australia retains a connection with this golden period of design thanks to the work of his understudy and design partner, Alex Russell, at Lake Karrinyup.

Russell arrived in Perth during 1928 fresh from designing Yarra Yarra and prior to heading back to Melbourne to build his magnum opus, the East Course at Royal Melbourne. Delighted with the quality of the Lake Karrinyup land at his disposal, Russell informed the club that, given the natural undulations and attractive surroundings, the course 'should compare favourably with any in Australia'. These words proved prophetic, with his outstanding course still widely regarded among the country's top few classics.

During the design stage, Russell made it clear that, where possible, blind shots into greens would be avoided, and although the course would be set up to challenge the scratch man, he hoped that for shorter hitters who could keep the ball straight it would not be overly taxing. Due to the severity of the undulations, however, achieving this playability proved difficult, with the designer conceding shortly after construction that his course was perhaps a little too tough. The main problem was that by restricting unsighted approach shots, his routing included a number of uphill drives, mostly bending left and favouring those with a strong draw. For the weaker players unable to reach the crest of these fairways, the side hill lies and partially concealed approach shots can be particularly nasty.

Russell did add that 'given good fairways to play second and third shots from, I think that you will find it fair and reasonable to all classes of golfers'. For their part the club maintains superb year round playing surfaces with the small, firm greens rolling truly and fiercely protected by classical bunkering and slippery contours. The couch fairways are also first class and at their best when left wide and free from the encumbrance of thick USGA

Long, tough and playing slightly uphill, the par three 8th at Lake Karrinyup.

style roughs areas, usually grown around tournament time to narrow the landing areas and make the battle one of attrition.

Peter Thomson and Michael Wolveridge, who have acted as course consultants since the early 1970s, helped strengthen the layout in recent years by adding more than twenty greenside and fairway bunkers and building nine new championship tees.

To keep pace with the modern professional game, they also pushed the 1st and 7th greens back by 50 metres and in the process took away the option to attack the driveable first hole for most players. This opening tee shot once set the tone for the entire round, with the hole tempting enough to entice golfers to have a crack but with serious repercussions for those not properly limbered up. With the existing traps restored and an additional set built beside the new green, the aggressive play is now virtually out of the question.

The second is where the course starts to grab your attention. The long hole rises from the tee before falling sharply at its dogleg, with a frightening blind downhill approach from a hanging lie for those who fail to reach the fairway peak. The most difficult holes on the course are those similarly built over the elevations with narrow landing areas, while the most interesting are the short, sloping par fours like the 9th, which rises toward the clubhouse, and the 10th, which descends down the hill in the opposite direction.

The beautifully bunkered 14th is now the shortest par four on the course and a particular favourite, offering the sort of risk/reward gamble that the first hole once did. The four intriguing par threes are also excellent, the clever greens holding only the most precise tee shots and testing a range of clubs.

The sweeping fairways and classical bunkering of Lake Karrinyup.

As the only course in the state to host a national Open, Karrinyup has enjoyed decades of recognition as the region's golfing jewel. A string of wonderful modern tracks, however, have brought unrivalled competition and threatened this existing order of ascendancy. Although no longer the undisputed top track, Lake Karrinyup does remain the West's best classic.

Joondalup Golf Resort

Course opened: Quarry and Dune 1985, Lake 1990
Designer: Robert Trent Jones Jr

Please forgive the outpouring of adjectives, but Joondalup is the most unique golf resort in Australia and in description the superlatives tend to flow. Built around an abandoned quarry, American designer Robert Trent Jones Jr brilliantly used the natural bush, dune and quarry landscapes to create 27 astonishing and totally absorbing golf holes.

The course is set out in three spectacular loops of nine, the Quarry, Dune and Lake, with each offering some of the most exhilarating challenges found on a golf course anywhere. The distinct terrain and unique design of each course makes it hard to compare Joondalup with other 18-hole courses, so I instead prefer to celebrate the resort as having Australia's three best nine-hole tracks. Although a little harsh on the original Quarry/Dune configuration, it's an appropriate tribute to the incredible diversity of each course.

The prominent features of the site are the magnificent cliff faces and limestone quarries, which actually come into play on each nine but are especially prominent on the wonderful Quarry course. The stunning par three 3rd is the most notorious hole, with a full carry of the enormous quarry required to avoid reloading. Visually intimidating from the tee, anything short or right is lost forever, while those who bail out to the left side of the 800 square metre green invariably end deep in three-putt territory.

'This special site produces one of the great golf courses in the game.'
Robert Trent Jones Jr

The 5th hole on Joondalup's incredible Quarry course.

No margin for error on the breathtaking Quarry 3 played straight over a gaping limestone quarry.

An amazing double dogleg par five follows, with the final third of its fairway played over and around an 80-metre sand hazard at the base of a 3-metre cliff. You need a ladder to climb into this bunker and a prayer to get out. The options for the second shot are to lay-up short of the sand or attack the cliff, the aggressive play needing to bite off enough of the hazard to reach a plateau fairway. The reward for the successful gamble is immense but the hazard colossal, making this one of the more exhilarating play-to-position shots in all of golf.

The most remarkable feature of the Dune course is its incredible elevation change, although it also includes a couple of awesome quarry holes. Once described as an 'overzealous mutation of parkland and links', the stomach tends to get a little queasy when driving down the massive roller coaster fairways, but the pumping heart can still appreciate the enormous scale of its design. The fourth is a long par three dropping severely from a cliff top with an elevated back 'Tiger' tee that comes highly recommended as it provides a stunning outlook over the greater Joondalup precinct. The view alone is worth the double bogey!

The more open and less dramatic Lake course was added to the roster in 1990. With glimpses of the Indian Ocean and the odd green open to a bump-and-run approach shot, it's almost a traditional links when compared to the other nines. In truth, the unusual mix of holes play nothing like a links, with man-made water hazards, flashes of the quarry and a series of adjacent holes featuring huge split fairways, extravagant bunkering and wickedly sloping greens. The tremendous short par four 2nd, set against a beautiful cliff, is the pick of the Lake holes.

Unless a total bandit, do not contemplate playing anywhere near your handicap on the first visit to Joondalup as all three courses are particularly brutal on newcomers. Steep tees and elevated greens with dipping fairways make correct club selection extremely difficult. Short balls often trickle off the greens and back down the fairway towards the frustrated golfer, while the enormous greens (up to ¼ of an acre) are heavily contoured with plenty of slippery breaks, so those who overcompensate on the approach usually leave themselves terrifying putts. With each round you learn more about the course and the challenge does get progressively easier.

Joondalup's tantalising combination of extravagant golf design, sumptuous five-star resort facilities and fabulous natural landscapes is irresistible and totally unforgettable. Described by its designer as 'unquestionably one of the world's finest golfing experiences', you will have to travel long and far before spotting anything on the planet that even remotely resembled the spectacular Joondalup resort.

The Vines Golf and Country Club, Lakes Course
Course opened: 1989
Designers: Graham Marsh, Ross Watson

Nestled in the famous wine-growing region of the Swan Valley and framed by the foothills of the Darling Ranges lies the highly rated and golf-driven Vines Resort. The resort's original developer allowed course designers Ross Watson and Graham Marsh to select the best available land from the site's 1000 acres with the resort, residential and country club facilities then built around the golf courses.

The Vines first opened as a 27-hole facility, with two of the nines forming a composite course, which has been regularly used as a professional tournament venue. When the fourth nine was added, in 1997 the current courses, Ellenbrook and Lakes, were created.

The latest nine forms part of the Ellenbrook course which touches the Ellenbrook Creek and has some major elevation changes, particularly on the older and more interesting back nine. As the name suggests, the Lakes Course incorporates several man-made water hazards, which feature most prominently on the famous finishing holes. Though many visit the Vines hoping to play the composite course, the Lakes alone is an excellent experience and well worth the trip.

Beautifully presented, the course sets up more like a traditional championship layout than a modern resort course with superb undulating couch fairways and beautifully contoured firm and fast bentgrass greens protected by strategic bunkering. Weaving initially through the rolling Australian bush and a wonderful array of native flowering trees and ancient grass trees, the round culminates in the dramatic closing holes built around the resort's main lakes.

Designer Ross Watson believes the most dominant feature of The Vines is the manner in which the course sits naturally into the site. 'It was framed at the outset by the native flora with much care taken not to disturb more ground than necessary', he says. The charming setting, traditional bunkering, firm surfaces and natural sandy base help give the course a classic Australian feel and make it one of the true golfing highlights of Western Australia.

The round starts off gently enough with two generous mid-length, well-bunkered par fours followed by a reachable par five, before the course bears its teeth at the tough 4th and 5th holes. Both have treacherous greens, the swales and hollows on the long par three 4th and the horseshoe-shaped 5th green being among the most extreme on either course.

The back nine has more signature moments with my highlight being the Sandbelt-style bunkering of the par four 11th hole. A line of sand down the left of the hole and a right side fairway lake creates an intimidating vista from the slightly raised tee, with the drive needing to avoid these hazards in order to set up the best approach into a narrow green protected by further traps and intricate mounding.

In true resort fashion, the par five finishing hole offers a grandstand all or nothing water carry to those searching for a last-gasp eagle, and has seen plenty of drama both in professional tournaments and social fourballs. Watson describes the hole as being 'right up there in the standout stakes. One must attack from the tee to set up a good chance to reach the par five green comfortably in two, which is not good enough in itself, as the green is huge with some very interesting contours'. A watery grave awaits any loose shot, but as the designer points out 'it's not a time to be "feint hearted"; as the "field" will be treating this more as a long par four, the pressure is on'.

Designed as a championship venue, the resort also sets up well for the average player with broad scale playability a key consideration. As Watson explains, 'The Vines fairways are for the most part reasonably generous and when using medium tee and pin locations the course sets up beautifully for a fun day played on some of the best turf in the country'. He adds that the 'holes were carefully designed to afford fun and challenge for the widest skill range and yet test the world's best tournament players. The firmness, tightness and bounce of the exquisite turf and the overall course presentation caps off a unique golfing experience of world standard'.

Meadow Springs Golf and Country Club

Course opened: 1987
Designer: Robert Trent Jones Jr

Prior to Meadow Springs I had played Trent Jones' four other Australian courses plus a handful in the United States and, after having been beaten up badly on each previous occasion, teed up at Meadow Springs with some trepidation.

My golf game was getting into good shape and the sole wish for the day was that the American would go easy on me and somehow leave a little dignity to take on my travels. After hitting a solid opening tee shot and a good six iron into the first green, I smirked as the eight-foot birdie putt got the day off to a good start. The smirk turned into a smile with a further birdie on the 2nd and jubilation with another on the 3rd. By the turn I'd added three more, shot the best nine hole score of my life and dismissed any thought of RTJ as a brutal oft-sadistic designer.

For the most part, Meadow Springs shows off the designer's mellow side with its challenging but fair design. Play well here and your score will reflect it. The grooming is impeccable with superb putting surfaces in a variety of shapes and sizes, plus immaculate couch fairways bending delightfully around large native trees and voracious fairway bunkers without cart paths to interrupt their beauty.

The first seven holes, carved through the open bushland, are the best on the course and rival any in Western Australia. The subtle undulation, classical bunkering and pure sand-based surfaces remind one of Melbourne's finest Sandbelt courses with each hole totally private and complete, with a vast array of native flora and fauna (kangaroos abound).

The nature of the land and composition of the residential development unfortunately dictated two significantly different nines, with the character of the course altering drastically from the 8th tee. From serene Sandbelt to pure resort, water hazards feature prominently on the next four holes. The 8th and 11th are remarkably similar mid-length par threes over ponds, while sandwiched between is a long hole with a water carry and a tricky short par four with a small slippery green best approached from close to the lake.

Set within a forest of towering gums, the uphill par four 17th features the trickiest green on the course.

There is a further change in character as the finishing holes play through an ancient tuart forest with towering 200 foot gums, dramatic elevation change and some trademark Trent Jones thrills and challenges. An example is the notorious uphill 17th with a wicked three-and-a-half tiered green that can turn the sweat into tears with one misjudged putt. If the pin is on the back shelf here, you may need to take an extra three clubs from the fairway!

Like his father, Robert Trent Jones Jr is a master of the extravagant, yet Meadow Springs is proof that he also has the ability to restrain this creative flair, moderate his design and create brilliant classical golf holes.

Secret Harbour Golf Links
Course opened: 1994
Designer: Graham Marsh

Any golfer lucky enough to have played at Spyglass Hill on California's Monterey Peninsula will recall the famous opening five holes, which are set among rugged coastal duneland alongside the Pacific Ocean. With the remaining thirteen holes inland and built within a surrounding forest, these celebrated sand dune holes are clearly the course's most memorable. For those wanting to experience something similar to the famous five at Spyglass, but unable to travel to Monterey, I suggest a visit to the Secret Harbour Golf Links south of Perth, particularly the first nine holes.

Secret Harbour was designed by Graham Marsh and opened its Links nine, now the back nine, in 1994, with developers selling housing sites around these holes at the same time as planning the second nine. In 1998, with the Links nine development complete, the Dunes nine was opened. While there are a number of exceptional holes on either nine, it is the towering, raw sandhills of the underdeveloped early holes that leave the greatest impression. The

The thrilling downhill drive on the 5th hole at Secret Harbour.

feeling of playing amid such huge dunes is a sensation new to Australian golfers, which, together with glimpses of the Indian Ocean, makes this section stand out.

Back-to-back long par fours at the 4th and 5th are the feature holes, with both beautifully built-in valleys between ridges of sand. Running adjacent to each other the holes play either into or with the usually stiff winds. The 4th is slightly uphill, with the drive needing to carry a large reed-filled swamp and pierce pot bunkers dotted throughout the fairway. It is not an easy driving hole as the sand behind the tee guards the wind whipping in from the coast. The 5th affords commanding views of a distant ocean with an exhilarating downhill tee shot to a narrowing and undulating fairway lined by bunkers that encroach the further the drive reaches. This green is one of the smallest on the course and protected by additional sand traps.

Sand, glorious sand—these dunes surrounding the par five 7th fairway will one day be covered in houses.

The older established back nine, with its holes encased by housing, is less impressive than the rugged beauty of the front side. The exception is the wonderful 15th, with the tee shot played through thick coastal shrub to a unique fairway dissected by a large bushcovered knoll. The options here are to drive around the knoll or lay-up and leave a long approach into an elevated, narrow green resting beneath a large sandy mound.

Though not a criticism of the design, it is unfortunate that the greater Secret Harbour community will eventually expand out to include home sites among the glorious front nine sand dunes. Although good enough to warrant a visit once this development is complete, the golfing purist is well advised to consider seeing this course prior to the hand of man interfering too much further.

Mt Lawley Golf Club
Course opened: 1929
Designer: David Anderson

Mt Lawley is an excellent private course located in Perth's northern suburbs on a beautiful tract of gently undulating sandy soil. The course was designed by Royal Perth professional David Anderson and opened in 1929.

With tight tree-lined fairways, traditional bunkering and firm, slick bent greens, this is a classical Sandbelt-style course in the mould of the nearby Lake Karrinyup Country Club. The fairway movement is less pronounced than at Karrinyup but well incorporated into the design with a number of fine driving holes over and across the slopes, the blind drive on the second being a particular favourite. Bunkering is a design feature with greenside traps cut close to putting surfaces that are generally subtle and mostly break off the shoulders of the bunkers.

The club's signature hole is the drop-kick par three 13th, named 'Commonwealth' after the shape of its green. Aerial photographs of this course from the early years are remarkable and show seventeen square greens and one resembling a map of Australia. The green no longer stands out as much, with the others changing over time, but its quirky shape can distract from what is a beautifully bunkered and contoured putting surface. Other highlights include the fine dogleg 12th hole and the tempting short par four 16th.

Though the odd hole is overplanted, the tremendous variety and superb year round conditioning helps Mt Lawley stand alongside Lake Karrinuyp as Perth's premier private club. If resort golf isn't your scene, then a trip to Perth should definitely include a round at both.

Albany Golf Club
Course opened: 1899
Designer: various

The coastal town of Albany in Western Australia's southwest was the first settled in the state and also houses its oldest golf course at the Albany Golf Club. The club has existed on its present site since 1899 when a group of locals built the nine hole links. It was not extended to 18 holes until 1963 and was reconfigured slightly in 2001 to accommodate a new clubhouse.

Situated among sandhills alongside a charming stretch of coastline that overlooks King George Sound, the course generally runs north–south and plays much longer than its

yardage due to hardy kikuyu fairways, which offer very little roll. The small greens are firm and fast, making approach play from the soft spongy fairways difficult to judge.

Aside from the fairway grasses, though, the course has an authentic links feel with natural bumps and undulation, small targets, modest pot bunkers and views of the adjacent beaches. The holes are lined by native 'Woolly' bushes, and when the offshore winds whip across the course, driving becomes very tight.

The standout stretch of holes is 11 through 13, which run directly alongside the sea and usually into the stiff prevailing winds. The 11th is a par five that dissects intruding tea-tree on either side of its narrowing fairway, while the 12th and 13th are classic par fours—dead straight, bunker free and with full views of the shore and nearby islands.

Albany is a delightful seaside town and the course an appropriate reflection of its charm and historic importance.

Araluen Country Club

Course opened: 1994
Designers: Michael Coate, Roger Mackay

Perched atop a plateau in the Roleystone Hills to the east of Perth, the Araluen Country Club is an incredible feat of construction and must have been close to the most difficult golf course in the country to build.

Set within a steep and secluded forest of towering natives, the course is built on a clay base of limestone and granite, with a red dusty rock lining each of the fairways. Designers Coate and Mackay did a fine job routing the course and shaping playable holes given such unsuitable settings.

The elevation change throughout is severe, with the steep holes seeming to play downhill much more frequently than uphill, which certainly would not have been possible without the compulsory golf cart. The most dramatic elevation drop comes at the short par three 16th, which falls almost 30 metres from tee to green. With a small creek in front of the target and thick forest behind, the hole is pretty, but judging the wind and selecting the right club is a matter of guesswork.

Mapped within the framework of a surrounding real estate development, a few holes feel a little integrated, with a number of greens seemingly set to provide eye-candy for potential investors. Most golfers, however, will enjoy the course with its broad fairways and large greens kept well-groomed and generally soft to ensure green fee players can handle their heavy contours. Despite its unfriendly base and severe topography, the designers have managed to create an interesting course among this forest of red rock and dust.

QUEENSLAND

Queensland is the Australian state most dominated by the modern golf course. Prior to the arrival of the foreign investment-driven resort boom of the 1980s, golf throughout Queensland was generally poor with fewer outstanding tracks than any another mainland state.

The capital's first club, Brisbane Golf Club was founded in 1896 and hosted every state amateur championship until a suitable alternative was found in 1927. Little wonder club members were irked when an infant Queensland Golf Club was afforded the Royal prefix ahead of it in 1923. The state's best classic, Royal Queensland, has also endured its share of misfortune, and though it lacks the visual grace of some of its Sydney or Melbourne counterparts, the course has long been underrated by southern golfers.

Queensland's most productive period of golf design began with the introduction of the resort game to Australia in the late 1970s at Kooralbyn Valley, which remains a fascinating design despite years of slow deterioration. South-east Queensland has subsequently grown to become Australia's resort golf capital with the Gold Coast, south of Brisbane, featuring our greatest concentration of resort courses and the magnificent Sunshine Coast to the north beginning to follow suit. Tropical North Queensland has also developed into an unlikely golf destination with the addition of some fine tracks, although the region is best visited during winter as the oppressive humidity can make summer golf this far north uncomfortable.

Modern Queensland highlights include the Greg Norman-designed The Grand and Brookwater which offer the best private and best Brisbane golf respectively. The wonderful Laguna Quays is a significant destination in itself, while the prolific design firm of Thomson, Wolveridge and Perrett have transposed their traditional style onto several properties with varying success, Hope Island remaining their finest work.

Golf in sunny Queensland is a direct contrast to the more traditional game played throughout the southern states, and though a little sanitised, its appeal is spreading. Carts have replaced buggies, a round has become an 'experience', and for their inflated green fee, golfers now demand, and receive, immaculate, lush green playing surfaces. Although the standard of Queensland golf has improved dramatically during this modern era, a large portion remains similarly styled which makes the diversity of its best tracks like The Grand, Laguna Quays, Glades, Hope Island, Royal Queensland and Brookwater all the more enjoyable.

Previous spread: The Grand Golf Club, 13th hole.

Below: The par three 16th hole at the Brookwater Golf Club south-west of Brisbane.

The Grand Golf Club

Course opened: 1997
Designers: Greg Norman, Bob Harrison

It is extremely rare for designers to be given two bites of the same design cherry, yet Queensland's fabulous Grand Golf Club exists as the second incarnation of Greg Norman's very first foray into golf course design. His association with the course actually started on the day his design company opened for business.

Originally known as the Gilston Golf Club, Norman and partner Bob Harrison had the course routed and ready for play by 1990, but unfortunately their Japanese client fell on hard times and abandoned the $30 million investment before a single divot could be taken. Left dormant for six years, it was overgrown and full of weeds when a consortium of frustrated local golfers bought the land, looking to establish an exclusive member's-only retreat free from the Gold Coast resort crowds. They chose an ideal site, as The Grand's greatest appeal is the peace and isolation of its natural and secluded hinterland setting.

With the course unrecognisable, the new owners looked to Norman and Harrison to restore it to its former unseen glory. The overgrowth was quickly cut away and one by one the golf holes rediscovered. Several landing areas were reshaped and all of the greens and bunkers remodelled, with the designers having significantly improved their artistic ability in this area during the ensuing years. After just 18 months, the course Mk II was ready for play, opening as The Grand and to almost instant acclaim.

Although not overly long, the track is certainly no pushover, with its short par fours and reachable par fives among the trickiest holes on the course, and the clever greenside contouring providing a stern examination of approach play and your powers of recovery. Those hoping to return a decent card must score well on the relatively easy opening holes, as the test gets progressively harder the further you travel.

The attractive bush setting of the par four 3rd hole at The Grand; to score well here you must make your birdies early.

The best section of holes starts with the par three 6th, played across the Nerang River, and runs through to back-to-back par fives at 11 and 12. These holes became infamous when the club was controversially selected by the AGU to host the 2001 Australian Open, a decision that was widely condemned and strangely damaging to the image of The Grand. The club had hoped, and supposedly paid, for a higher profile, yet the fact the course produced a quality tournament, worthy winner and looked spectacular almost escaped notice and certainly failed to impress sections of the media and a number of disgruntled marquee professionals.

Admittedly, the 11th was a disaster with the hole shortened to play as a par four but the landing area so sharply sloped that even the best tee shots kicked into rough and left an impossible approach over a pond to a small green that would not hold. Following the tournament, this fairway slope was softened. The legitimate problems with this hole, however, seemed to provide ammunition to extend complaints unfairly to other parts of the course.

The highly original par five 12th was another major sore point with the players, many of whom got wet searching for eagles by bending approach shots around the large gums protecting the middle of the green. Despite plenty of fairway to the side of the water, the professional instinct was to go for glory regardless of the percentages of the shot or the positioning of their drives. High numbers left dented egos which led to a chorus of discontent, yet what they failed to recognise was that these were the shots and options that separated the good from the great and were precisely what the paying public had come to see.

Along with the similarly controversial short par four 10th and its wicked green, these holes are the most interesting and attractive on the course, with anything from an eagle to a double bogey a real possibility.

The view from behind the controversial but enjoyable par five 12th; note the trees in the centre of the fairway.

Many of those who chastise The Grand have not actually had the pleasure of a game here, so don't believe everything you read because despite hiccups as an Open venue, there is not a track like this anywhere in Queensland. Challenging, charming, ultra-exclusive and always presented in mint condition, this is one course definitely worth grovelling to play.

Laguna Quays Resort, Turtle Point Golf Course

Course opened: 1992
Designers: David Graham, Gary Panks

Built by a Japanese shipping company in the early 1990s, the magnificent five-star Laguna Quays Resort is set amongst almost 2000 hectares of sublime coastal bushland along Queensland's stunning Great Barrier Reef. An unspoilt paradise with a constant outlook over the beautiful Whitsunday Coast, the resort also comes complete with a superb 18 hole golf course.

The par five 14th hole at Laguna Quays, which runs alongside the waters of the Whitsundays.

Designed by two-time major winner David Graham and American architect Gary Panks, the course and its most famous hole, the seaside 6th, are named after the outcrop behind the tee known as Turtle Point, where the turtles of the region annually come to mate. Taking golfers on a magical journey through bush and virgin rainforest, the course affords glimpses of the Barrier Reef and even runs alongside the tropical waters of Repulse Bay.

After a comfortable opening things start to get interesting at the 5th, which bends through thick bush towards a large green set beneath a crop of spectacular rainforest. The dense growth can be disorientating, but as you head to the next hole, the forest suddenly opens up to present the glorious islands of the Whitsunday passage in full view from the 6th tee. A rock wall runs down the entire left side of the hole to separate you from the water, but nothing can interrupt this breathtaking vista. With the wind whipping in from the islands, golfers need to start their tee shot close to the sea as an enormous bunker, that doubles as a cart path, runs the entire length of the fairway to catch the not-so-brave who bail too far to the right.

Tantalisingly the course then heads back inland with the coastal holes, for now, left behind. The next sea glimpse comes when standing on the 13th tee and is even more memorable, especially for first timers. The long par three heads straight from the forest towards the

Reef and an enormous green framed by the islands that lurk in the distance. The final signature hole is the par five 14th which runs alongside the sea in much the same manner as the 6th hole. Interestingly, both were built on reclaimed land with more than half of the earth excavated to build the entire course used to form these two holes.

Golf at Laguna Quays isn't all about views though, with a tremendous variety of holes playable to resort golfers and thoroughly enjoyable for the single figure marker. Aside from the 13th, the lily pond 4th and water carry 11th are also excellent short holes, while the 12th is a great par five and, together with 11, 13 and 14, forms part of the best stretch on the course.

Though less dramatic, the closing holes are also very potent with the reachable par four 17th armed with water long and left for the overcooked hook and deep bunkers short and right to catch the weak block. Bending right up a steep hill, the tough 18th is another fine hole and a fittingly finale to an unforgettable round.

The whole Turtle Point experience is first-class with an exceptional design and awesome views complemented by phenomenal playing surfaces. Tees and fairways are a perfect carpet of the 328 Bermuda grass usually reserved for greens in this part of the world, and at their best are superior to any in Queensland. The large putting surfaces are suitably subtle for the resort traffic they receive, while the bunkering is strategic and features a number of gigantic hazards shaped to thrill. I'm not certain why David Graham's passion for golf design waned after this project, but on evidence of his work here, a successful career was sacrificed.

My first visit to the resort lasted all of 20 hours yet included three rounds of golf. The beauty of the setting and incredible conditioning of the golf course left an indelible impression and, like most, I immediately starting planning my next visit to this tropical paradise. The perfect resort for golfers and non-golfers alike, if you haven't played Turtle Point, don't even think about planning your next golf trip without carefully considering Laguna Quays.

The Glades Golf Club

Course opened: 2000
Designers: Greg Norman, Bob Harrison

When the Glades opened towards the end of 2000, it was to an unprecedented level of interest and critical acclaim. It appeared an increasingly discerning Gold Coast market wanted a break from the standardised US-style resort course and instead sought a championship test within an attractive natural sanctuary.

In fact the Glades land was originally a flat, featureless dairy farm entirely covered in kikuyu when an ambitious Korean with a dream armed Greg Norman Golf Design with a generous budget and a brief to build the best golf course possible. This proved especially difficult as the site was located within flood plains and local authorities insisted that its capacity to store floodwater be retained. To offset the residential areas which had to be built up, the golf course was constructed between one and two metres below its previous ground level with a delicate balance of cut and fill required to meet the project's aesthetic and technical requirements. As a result and surprising to most, every feature of the golf course is artificial, the outcome of what designers choose to do with their empty canvas.

'It's interesting that most people think that we were lucky enough to inherit all of these wetlands before building our golf course. In a way that's a nice compliment, but the reality is very different.'

Bob Harrison

The remarkably natural looking Norman/Harrison wetlands to the right of the par five 12th green.

The central feature of the design are the wetlands, all nine hectares of them, which spread throughout the site to enhance the course and contrast the lush playing surfaces. They also serve an environmental purpose with the region now alive and thriving with an abundance of waterfowl and birdlife. To help these, hand-drawn hazards appear as totally natural bodies of water, the designers used images from wetland books as references, planting reeds and

scattering dead trees throughout the murkied waters for effect. Some logs were laid in the water, and others planted vertically to make them look like they had died in place. Despite each tree costing around $5000, designer Bob Harrison recalls that the client, initially shocked by the cost, 'eventually embraced the idea and we ended up with dead trees everywhere'.

As one would expect, the standout holes are those which incorporate these wetlands. Many are shaped around the water and angled to provide an optimum line of approach for those running the gauntlet from the tee. An exception is the outstanding 2nd hole which cuts around a lake with its green actually titled towards the outside of the fairway. The long closing hole, however, is the classic example of a hazard that should be attacked, as the narrow green becomes either unreachable or virtually unholdable to those who drive too far away from the water.

Another highlight is the 16th green, which is delicately angled to reward the aggressive line alongside or across the water from the tee, with an approach free from the encumbrance of gaping sand traps and sharp slopes. In this country, water carry par threes don't come any prettier than the 17th hole at the Glades. The short iron from an island tee to the peninsula green is played across the most secluded section of wetlands with a shallow target dangling enticingly on the very edge of dry land.

The greens at Glades are exceptional and generally raised for protection from the more severe floods. Surfaces are turfed with the finest A4 bentgrass, which explains why pampered southerners feel particularly at home here. Cleverly contoured, these greens are hard, fast and guarded by strategic bunkering and clever swales, usually on opposing sides of the targets. Norman himself likes this balance and believes the greenside undulation allows a good player with feeling in his hands to get up and down from almost anywhere. He says that 'the fact some greens are elevated actually helps the concept. The average player is not penalised by barbed wire rough on the immediate green surrounds and can even putt out of some of the hollows'.

Sadly the Korean developer fell upon hard times in the 1990s and the course sat dormant for three years before a consortium purchased the site, added the finishing touches and completed the concept. Despite its humble beginnings, the Glades is an Australian original and a stark reminder of what a great imagination and fanatical attention to design detail can overcome.

Brookwater Golf Club

Course opened: 2002
Designers: Greg Norman, Bob Harrison

I first saw Brookwater when still under construction, and aside from being awe-struck by the beauty of its forest setting, my lasting memory was of crashing a golf cart down a steep embankment onto the freshly sodded 8th green and shattering the windscreen. Returning from my site tour battered and bruised, I suspected that this would some day seem an appropriate introduction to this difficult but exhilarating golf course.

From a golfing perspective, the first look at Brookwater is equally memorable. Situated within an enchanting nature reserve, its beauty is overwhelming and the design among the most compelling of this modern era. Incredibly, the course was the first built within the Brisbane area since the 1970s, and despite its infancy is clearly the city's top track.

As part of a residential subdivision, the golf course contains a lot of single holes that will eventually be flanked by the housing development. The overriding objective throughout the project, however, was to preserve as much of the bush as possible in order to provide an attractive setting for golf and to ensure that even when the estate is fully developed, the housing will be barely noticeable. As a result the fairway corridors were kept deliberately narrow with the designers not wanting to remove a single tree more than necessary and choosing instead to shape the landing areas to play more forgiving.

Built through rolling forests of established ironbarks and other tall eucalypts, the holes run along valleys, steep gullies and up and over ridges with trouble lurking on either side of the enclosed fairways. The extremely undulating nature of the site lent itself to the design team's preferred method of classic style MacKenzie-esque bunkering. Bob Harrison stresses this was not done out of reverence to the great man but because 'it makes the most sense if you believe in creating golf holes which look good as well as being interesting to play'. The bunkering is big and bold with steep faces cleverly contoured to dominate the vistas and blend naturally into surroundings. Hours were spent on site with excavators setting out the shapes and then trimming and refining after the first cut so that each bunker was not only practical but looked exciting.

Stirring start—the awesome opening tee shot at Brookwater.

Like MacKenzie and Morcom a lifetime before them, bunkering has become the Norman/Harrison trademark. Artistic yet set within the parameters of the design's philosophy, the hazards here are even more commendable considering the site's unsuitable clay base. Importantly though, the layout is also outstanding with a tremendous set of short holes and a number of mid-length par fours and reachable par fives that give golfers of any ability the opportunity to score well. Despite wild fairway movement and sharp elevation change, the course manages to remain playable from the social plates, and is a special treat for low markers from the very back.

Sun streaming through the trees on the par five 13th; note the bold bunkering and built-up fairway edges.

Brookwater has quickly become an Australian classic and had the pair not outdone themselves at Ellerston, would rank up with Royal Canberra as our premier inland course. While I'm sure your first experience will be less dramatic than mine, I am also quite certain that Brookwater will leave a lasting impression.

Hope Island Golf Club

Course opened: 1993
Designers: Peter Thomson, Michael Wolveridge, Ross Perrett

Following on from the success of their shaped links at Twin Waters came Hope Island and the opportunity for Peter Thomson and Michael Wolveridge to repeat the dose, this time for a prominent Japanese client with an enormous budget. The client, Mr Isutani, had purchased a dairy farm on the Gold Coast that was flat and devoid of natural feature and located over marine clays. As Wolveridge explains, he 'naturally wanted the best course in Australia and though we indicated the land was poor, he replied the budget was good and suggested we do a links course like Twin Waters. We jumped at the chance to do another manufactured links'.

Hope Island was an enormous project with the entire 50-hectare site raised at least two metres to protect the course from flooding. When a good clay deposit was found alongside the 18th fairway, some 1.2 million cubic metres was mined to build the links, leaving an enormous lake more than 20 metres deep. The clay was then overlaid with sand dredged from the nearby Coomera River. The arduous task of laying these foundations was vital to the concept's eventual success, with the designers then able to build fairways with hard, running undulation without the fear of sodden grasses. They were also able to shape the landscape with an unlimited imagination, and to encourage a natural links appearance on a very unnatural site.

The result is remarkable, showcasing the finest elements of traditional design with the course looking like, and more importantly playing like, a classic links despite its sub-tropical setting. An abundance of water may disturb staunch aficionados, but the thick tussocks of rough, penal pot bunkering, large moderate greens and beautifully crafted humps and hollows throughout the wide fairways help to create that genuine British feel. The traditional style works especially well on the opening holes where there are few interruptions from a bustling outside world. An integrated residential resort built around parts of the back nine, while unobtrusive, can be slightly distracting.

'An instant links was born.'
Michael Wolveridge

The view from behind the 18th green on the Hope Island links.

*Hope Island's 2nd hole,
the first of two very
good front nine par fives.*

Despite several wonderful moments, the par fives, each tackling the wind from a different angle, are the highlight and the best set of three shot holes the team has built. The first two are especially memorable, with the 2nd bending around a lake but otherwise an authentic links hole with wonderfully positioned pot bunkers and a raised green of immense proportions. The 8th is another cracking five where the mighty can get home in two but along the way must avoid a series of devilishly tough bunkers that were inspired by the Principal's Nose at St Andrews.

On the back nine, the huge hazard down the left side of the long 18th dominates the finish to the round, although keeping dry is not your only concern with more than eleven pot bunkers waiting to catch anything too ambitious. Other standout holes include the wetlands hole at 13 and the bump and run par four 15th. The long water carry par three 17th, which takes you from St Andrews to Sawgrass, is a throw back to the sort of resort golf you'll find elsewhere on the Gold Coast but a minor blemish on an otherwise brilliant canvas.

Hope Island is living proof of the fickleness of public perception, having ridden a roller coaster of critical acclaim and analysis since a stunning opening back in 1993. Initially hailed as the nation's greatest resort course, the industry seemed to turn cold when the resort struggled to cope with maintenance issues born of its humid environment. A change of ownership in 2000 brought a renewed resolve to restore the standard of course conditioning, with particular focus on the greens. All eighteen were re-surfaced with a more robust 328 Bermuda grass, and the new fast and true surfaces are again among the best on the Coast.

With all their success subsequent to this project and despite the featureless site given, for me, the outstanding 'instant links' at Hope Island remains Thomson and Wolveridge's greatest achievement.

Hyatt Regency Coolum Golf Course

Course opened: 1988
Designer: Robert Trent Jones Jr

The Hyatt Regency Resort at Coolum on the Sunshine Coast is home to one of the finest resort golf experiences in Australia. It is a 160-hectare subtropical paradise situated minutes from the beautiful beaches of Queensland's magnificent Sunshine Coast. With all the first class amenities you expect from a five-star resort, the sculptured and lush golf course remains Coolum's showpiece and a wonderful contrast to the natural beauty of the region. Designed by the enigmatic Robert Trent Jones Jr, Coolum represents one of his more subtle designs with the usual resort golf thrills and challenges but minus the signature Trent Jones trickery.

The layout is not overly long, with the longest par four measuring 390 metres and only one other over 370 metres, but makes up for any lack of length with a brilliant combination of contrasting landscapes. Holes are carved out of the region's swampland, around a series of man-made lakes and through forests of tall natives. The challenge therefore lies in mastering the variety of holes and hazards found throughout the course, from links to lakes and marshland to bushland.

Each distinct landscape is wonderfully used with the best moments spread evenly between both nines. The five holes on the beach side of the highway, 4 through 8, are built around the area's swamps with long reeds growing out of the marsh to make the hazards seem even more intimidating. The signature hole here is the stunning par three 6th, set against the backdrop of Mount Coolum and played directly over calf high rough and snake infested wasteland. According to Aboriginal legend, Mount Coolum was formed by the watching gods after a young warrior, Coolum, had been slain while courageously fighting for a beautiful maiden. Many golfers have shared the Coolum heartbreak as they, too, gallantly battle for the most beautiful maiden of all, a birdie two on this inspiring hole.

From the 8th Trent Jones takes us back to the main property where the odd hole is shaped out of the bushland but the majority crafted around the resort's lakes. One impressive hole dominated by the water is the elevated all-carry par three 11th, which is

Coolum's treacherous
one shot 11th hole.

played to a bean-shaped green bending around the lake. The bail out area to the left leaves a frightening chip back towards the water, so the best option is to take a deep breath, fly at the pin and enjoy the challenge.

The strong 18th is another fine hole played around the water and the scene of many a dramatic final hole collapse, especially when pins are cut close to the hazard. From the tee, the optimum line is adjacent to the lake as fairway bunkers line the outside of the dogleg and the brave tee shot sets up a much clearer approach into the small green. Trent Jones once described Coolum as 'not designed to punish the champions, just to find out who they are'. The course though is tough, and walk off this final hole with a decent score and you will certainly feel like a champion.

Pelican Waters Golf Club

Course opened: 2000
Designers: Greg Norman, Bob Harrison

Pelican Waters is situated at the southern tip of Queensland's gorgeous Sunshine Coast and is surrounded by national parks and an unspoilt creek system. Though several kilometres inland from the famous coastline, the golf course retains a sense of the region's beauty, with its diverse landscapes and crafted wetlands cleverly incorporated into the design. Holes initially weave around open areas of low-lying scrub and later through tall stands of native bush with the ever-present lake system a constant companion.

Like the Glades, much of this course's visual appeal is the result of the improvisation of designers Norman and Harrison. Here their flat canvas had an unusual twist with a clay-based northern section and an attractive sandy heathland southern section that flowered prolifically for several months each year. Once the water bodies had been created, the excavators actually shifted tonnes of this sandy material over the entire finished golf course shape. The native grasses then grew back, virtually unassisted, to form the natural roughs that now frame the groomed areas, working especially well leading in and out of hazards.

The classical bunkering is a feature of the design with the sand found on site helping to build bunkers with dark, vertical faces. These are essentially Sandbelt in style; the difference, however, is that the designers like to see wilderness growing out of the sides of their bunkers, and by using the vegetation were able to create a number of wasteland hazards, some even extending all the way to the water's edge. These stunning beaches of sand are particularly prominent on the first two par fives and the beautiful par three 14th.

Despite being well-endowed with a number of challenging long holes, Pelican Waters' greatest strength is its short par fours. The 2nd is a superb example of strategic design with water running across the tee and up the right side of the hole, tempting the bold player to take a risk. The longer the club, the more water to carry to reach the fairway, and if successful, the easier the pitch onto an angled green, with its series of left side bunkers impeding only those who choose to lay-up.

An outstanding example of the wasteland bunkering at Pelican Waters, here at the par three 14th sprawling all the way to the water's edge.

The other standout is the brilliantly deceptive 12th, which Harrison rates as one of the best short fours the team has ever built. It is certainly the most intricate, as there is ample width off the tee, yet parts of the sharply contoured green are hidden beyond a mound if approached from the wrong side of the fairway. The back pins are especially difficult to get near unless the drive can hug the fairway traps. Like the 2nd, the brave drive here is rewarded with an ideal angle of approach and a genuine chance at birdie. Visually this hole is particularly pleasing, considering the land was initially dead flat and the rolling terrain now appears so natural that many consider the firm lucky to have 'found' such a wonderful knoll to slot the green behind.

The finish to the round is extremely strong, with the final four holes played back through dense bushland. The par five 16th is a great hole that bends and meanders through chutes of tall gums which seem to narrow as you near the small target. The 17th is another difficult dogleg, while those who reach the 18th and relax are suitably punished by one of the toughest closing holes in Queensland. Take four here and you are likely to be signing an impressive scorecard.

Although the design team has had better land to work with, this largely unheralded course deserves to be duly recognised as one of the state's top modern tracks. The contrasting native bush and heath landscapes are complemented by the rugged nature of design, which gives the course a rough edge that is uncommon throughout Queensland. Far from your typical resort course, Pelican Waters is an original and one that would work just as well without the expectation of immaculate playing surfaces and the convenience of carts and red carpet resort service. Not that the perfect lush lies and lavish amenities are a problem, but the real pleasure at Pelican is in combating the natural features of the site and mastering its constant unpredictability.

The brilliantly shaped 12th green and surrounds; from flat ground into one of Australia's best modern short par fours.

Sanctuary Cove Resort, Pines Course

Course opened: 1989
Designer: Arnold Palmer

The 470-hectare resort at Sanctuary Cove was Australia's first fully integrated tourist resort and built around four man-made harbours on the Gold Coast's picturesque Coomera River. As well as several hundred private residences, the resort also boasts two golf courses, a waterfront marine village, five-star Hyatt Regency hotel and a 300-berth marina.

Of the golf courses, the acclaimed Pines Course is the highlight. Designed by golfing great Arnold Palmer, the course achieved instant recognition when the resort's owners brought the Australian Skins game and high-profile Sanctuary Cove Classic to the new layout in the early 1990s. Measuring almost 6700 metres with an abundance of water, the course stretched the professionals and received an unheard of AGU rating of 76. Although course ratings four shots above par have become more widespread, the Pines first took penal design to this new level and remains one of the toughest courses in the country.

The course is carved through a pine forest, which appears natural but was in fact planted by the developers as part of the Pines Course concept. The routing weaves through the stands of trees and around six large man-made lakes, in play on fourteen of the holes to ensure there is no let-up from the constant pressure.

Following a relatively benign opening, the brain is given a rest while the brawn takes over and tries to tackle a terrifying stretch of golf from the 8th through the 11th. Two unreachable par fives, both over 530 metres, and two monster par fours (over 430 metres) equal more than 1960 metres of heartbreak. Anyone taking less than twenty shots to play these four holes has done extremely well.

The 10th is notorious as perhaps the most intimidating hole in the entire country with water running down the right side of its narrow fairway and a pine forest down the left. There is simply no substitute for a long straight drive on this hole as anything less equals an instant bogey at best! The approach shot is also perilous, with a surprisingly small green protected by water and generally attacked with a long iron or fairway wood.

The all-or-nothing par three 13th on the Pines Course at Sanctuary Cove.

There are many ways the Pines can ruin your scorecard. It can slowly destroy with its relentless pressure, or punish savagely on holes like the infamous 13th where a full 200-metre plus water carry is required to reach the island green. The long 18th hole, around the lake, is another severe test and an appropriate climax to the thrills and spills that precede it. To have any chance of getting to the small green in two, the tee shot must skirt the water down the left side of the fairway, and while a par here is a tremendous achievement, those struggling through the first seventeen holes will be happy just to avoid a soggy ball on this difficult finale.

As part of a wonderful resort, the challenge of the Pines and the exceptional presentation of both courses make Sanctuary Cove well worth the visit for all Gold Coast bound golfers.

Paradise Palms Golf Course
Course opened: 1990
Designers: Graham Marsh, Ross Watson

The approach to the 10th green is fraught with danger as both the putting surface and lake are hidden from the fairway.

Tropical North Queensland is the world's leading reef and rainforest destination, where two pristine World Heritage wonders meet along a tropical coastline. Sculpted by Mother Nature and marketed by man, the region is also rapidly developing into a quality golf destination, offering a series of modern resort-style courses built to accommodate an increasing number of golf starved tourists. With travelling golfers now seeking a holiday that offers distractions away from the course, the rich bounties of North Queensland and the Barrier Reef are an obvious attraction.

In golfing terms, Paradise Palms is the region's heavyweight. Tough and uncompromising, the course was built on a former cane plantation wedged between World Heritage Rainforest and the Great Barrier Reef. The beautiful mountains of the Dividing Ranges provide a stunning backdrop to most holes, with fairways lined by dense stands of eucalypts and lush tropical rainforest. Also waiting to confiscate stray balls are the six main lakes and a number of meandering creeks, many dissecting fairways, that come into play on at least ten holes.

The brief to designers Marsh and Watson was to create Australia's most difficult tournament venue with the test starting at the long double dogleg first hole. Any thoughts of a gentle opener are quickly brushed aside, with the hole bordered by a thick copse, split by a creek and especially tough on those not fully warmed up. The par three 7th hole is the most spectacular on the front nine with panoramic views of the Dividing Ranges and the Reef's Clifton Beach from the elevated 'Taipan' tees. Slicers beware: anything slightly right here is certain to get wet, as the tee shot must clear a slender stream that feeds a small pond to the right of an incredibly narrow green.

On the back nine the largest lake on the course dominates the daunting 10th hole which initially heads uphill and measures in excess of 540 metres from the very back. Water runs down the right side of the hole with the second shot, played blind over a rise, needing to be precise as the fairway slopes towards the hidden water hazard. Closing the round is the adjacent par five 18th, which features stunning 180-degree views of the distant mountain ranges and a huge green typical of the putting surfaces found throughout the course.

Covering a total of 10,000 square metres, most greens are long and narrow and play tighter than their size would suggest. The steep slopes can make recovery tough with little green area to use and plenty of bumps and hollows to affect the chip shot. Playing surfaces are generally first-class, although serious golfers are well advised to visit during the cooler months to see this course in its best shape as oppressive summer humidity can badly affect turf quality.

Course designer Ross Watson describes Paradise Palms as 'a five-star tropical experience'. He adds, 'the course is always presented beautifully and the intrinsic challenge is always there, freshened by the ever present Whitsunday Doctor [ocean breezes] which springs up on most days'.

Lakelands Golf Club

Course opened: 1997
Designer: Jack Nicklaus

Lakelands was the first Jack Nicklaus course to open in Australia following his famous redesign of The Australian Golf Club during the 1970s. Built on a flat seasonal floodplain, the original developer's vision was to transform an uninteresting site into a world-class golf course, in harmony with the natural balance of its sensitive environment.

The results were very pleasing with the fully public championship layout proving an excellent addition to the Gold Coast golf scene, and regarded in many quarters as the best-conditioned resort course in Australia. Add the wonderful practice facilities, luxurious clubhouse and service excellence of Clubcorp management, and Lakelands becomes a first-class, five-star golf experience.

As the name implies, there is plenty of water on the course with a carefully constructed lakes system blending seamlessly with its surrounding landscape and built to add visual interest to the design. Though visible from many holes, the water only features prominently on a handful, the most noticeable being the attractive 'signature' par three 14th. Playing little more than a wedge, the tight target is protected by a pond and split-level waterfall. The hole takes a great picture but could have used a few extra metres, especially on the back tee.

The view from behind Lakeland's 8th green.

After a steady opening, the course starts to get interesting from the 7th hole, an excellent short par four with a clever plateau green. The next is a wonderful hole with a lone directional bunker in the centre of a deceptive, dipping fairway that hides part of a lake from the tee. Correct club selection is absolutely vital, both off the tee and on the approach, which is over the edge of the water and into a shallow kidney-shaped green. The mid-length 10th

is the hole that makes best use of the lakes as a strategic hazard by rewarding those who can drive close to the water from the tee with a much easier approach.

Well bunkered throughout, the course has a classic Nicklaus feel with expanses of wasteland fairway bunkers mixed with the carefully contoured and artistic greenside traps. Thick tussocks of rough are often used within or around the huge fairway bunkers to help define the hazards.

In keeping with Nicklaus' design philosophies, the course caters to golfers of all standards with a choice of five tee options, each said to have been personally tested by the Golden Bear himself. The course grooming, year round, has been outstanding, with perfect Windsor Green couch fairways and hardy Bermuda-strain Tifdwarf greens that have become firmer and truer with each passing year. Aesthetically, the casuarinas planted extensively throughout the course have helped to obstruct the Surfers Paradise skyline and create a haven for golfers to enjoy their round.

Even if the more sanitised resort game is not usually to your liking, it is easy to appreciate the attraction of the Lakelands experience. Impeccably presented and immaculately groomed, the course pampers guests with its extraordinary playing surfaces, first-class service and superb amenities.

Capricorn International Golf Resort, New Course
Course opened: 1992
Designer: Karl Litten

Part of the Rydges International Resort on Queensland's beautiful tropical Capricorn Coast, the Karl Litten designed New Course is a searching examination of your golf game and one of the more interesting resort courses in Queensland.

Unlike most of its contemporaries, the challenge here isn't about keeping your ball dry, though there is the usual splattering of water; rather it's about combating the stands of tall trees that line fairways and mark the doglegs. With the exception of just two holes, the par fours and fives all bend around natural lakes and lagoons and through the thick melaleuca bush. Subtle undulation changes and tight tree-lined corners often make the holes seem narrower and the preferred target harder to pinpoint from the tee. This visual deception not only makes the New Course tough, but also very interesting.

Beginning with three difficult long holes, the course then moves to the memorable fourth with a notorious diagonal bunker running for at least 150 metres across the hole,

some 240 metres from the tee. Drives will generally stay well short of the hazard, leaving a long iron approach, slightly uphill, to a generous green.

The back nine is the highlight with a number of fine holes including the water carry par three 11th, and the funky par four 13th, with its stunning downhill approach shot played over palms trees and across a lagoon. The par five 15th is also unique with a lake and no fewer than fifteen fairway bunkers running the entire left-hand side of the hole. To set up an eagle putt, the brave golfer must flirt with the hazard from the tee and then carry sand and water on an exhilarating approach.

The pick of the holes, however, is the difficult 17th, which looks innocuous but is far from gentle on the unsuspecting golfer. A classic tight driving hole, the fairway bends around tall trees and a lake that runs down the left and guards the green. The natural tendency to play away from the corner has dire consequences here, as further trees on the far side of the fairway impede the approach and force golfers to play a fade out over the water to bend the ball back onto the green.

For the not-so-brave, the New Course has bail out options but never all-inclusive relief, and as a result course management is vital to low scoring. This is far from your typical 'grip it and rip it' resort course, with correctly judging the angles of fairways and trees pivotal to approach play. Local knowledge can be a huge advantage but is totally worthless if you are unable to execute the shots you know you need to make.

As prolific American designer Karl Litten's only Australian course, Capricorn New is a fascinating break from the standard resort fare thrown up at countless other courses around Queensland, and for that sole reason, well worth a look by serious and social golfers alike.

Novotel Twin Waters Resort Golf Course
Course opened: 1990
Designers: Peter Thomson, Michael Wolveridge

Queensland's Sunshine Coast, an area of unsurpassed beauty north of Brisbane, is rapidly expanding into one of the country's finest golf destinations. The Twin Waters golf course is one of the region's original championship courses and was built during resort golf's boom days of the late 1980s. Together with the nearby Hyatt Coolum resort, which opened in 1988, Twin Waters helped to bring serious golfers to this unspoiled coastal paradise in search of great golf.

The course itself is a fascinating study of the desires of design partners Michael Wolveridge and Peter Thomson to impose their design style on a rugged and naturally Australian landscape. Heavily influenced by the classic British links, the design is unashamedly traditional and one of the clearest examples of their unmistakable style.

Despite the resort setting and warm humid climate, the philosophies of links golf have been fully integrated into the layout, making an interesting if not totally coherent challenge. Running approach play is encouraged through design, yet the surfaces are also receptive to attacking 'target' golf. The beautiful native flora and fauna of the site also offer a distinctly Australian slant on the ancient game: nowhere else are your bump and run shots likely to be so carefully watched by galleries of kangaroos.

Many physical characteristics of the British game are evident, including gently rolling fairways, small wicked pot bunkers, patches of thick tussock rough and large firm greens with subtle slopes. There are the usual water hazards and lush green fairways synonymous with resort golf, but the more traditional elements provide a nice contrast.

Embracing the adage that golf is a game for all seasons and all players, the course is not difficult to walk, nor is it overly taxing on that new box of balls in your bag. The playing surfaces are always superb and with the Novotel's fine resort facilities on hand, Twin Waters is not a course to miss while visiting the glorious Sunshine Coast.

'Twin Waters was the first links-style course to be constructed in Australia and, in a sense, remains my favourite. It contains so many subtleties and is always interesting to play. The uncharacteristic presence of lakes was unavoidable as they provided the necessary fill to build the course. Eventually their acidic qualities reduced and they became a pleasant habitat for wildlife and to granting golfers a cooling effect on warm days.'
Michael Wolveridge

An unlikely mix—resort bunkering and links mounding on the 8th fairway at Twin Waters.

The Links Golf Club, Port Douglas

Course opened: 2000
Designers: Peter Thomson, Michael Wolveridge, Ross Perrett

Links golf and the hot, humid North Queensland climate are an interesting and unlikely combination. While some love the mix, others feel it a little contrived. Personally, the concept reminds me of the impressions of American golf architecture in Scotland and Ireland. Read reviews of the New Ballybunion course and you'll appreciate why. Many think it's the greatest aberration in golf while others believe the Trent Jones Jr creation to be the equal of the famous Old Course.

The Links at Port Douglas is the world's first tropical links and a fascinating example of traditional design within the hostile Queensland tropics. Located close to Port Douglas' famous Four Mile beach, the 73-hectare sandy stretch adjacent to the Coral Sea was a former cane farm and features gorgeous mountain vistas and a stunning rainforest backdrop. Though the site was far from the ideal base with which to replicate the British links, designer Michael Wolveridge persisted. He explains that 'we found consistent evidence of ancient coral reef life which encouraged me to create an authentic links, restoring the farmed land to small sand dunes and an open landscape more akin to Scotland than the tropics. Cooled by an ever-present sea breeze, seasonal winds brought traditional links challenge with their weighty might'.

A number of classic links elements have been incorporated into the design including a double green, blind targets, hidden pot bunkers and even a small burn crossing the 6th green. Typically large and well protected, the greens are surrounded by humps and hollows and built in the image of St Andrews. As Wolveridge says, 'they are large and firm with uncomplicated putting, but the very devil to get on'.

The course starts alongside its beautiful Queenslander clubhouse, and bends towards an ample green with views out to the more open and exposed fairways of the front nine. The back nine is split by a curtain of pristine rainforest that runs through the centre of the site, effectively dividing the links and reminding golfers that they are in fact still in the tropics.

Port Douglas is a sensational holiday destination with a treasure-trove of bounties to explore. The new Links Golf Club is yet another first class distraction for holiday makers, although best tackled during the cooler winter months when the humidity is less crushing, and the turf more receptive to the hard and fast running game so typical of the ancient links.

The Kooralbyn Resort Golf Course

Course opened: 1979
Designer: Desmond Muirhead

Situated near Beaudesert, an hour from both Brisbane and the Gold Coast, Kooralbyn was the first course to introduce compulsory cart golf to Australia and one of the pioneering resorts that helped drive the Queensland golf revolution of the 1980s.

Designed by English architect Desmond Muirhead, the course is truly unique with holes routed through and across a series of valleys and hills providing plenty of interesting elevation change and attractive rural views. Though full of exciting moments, two holes stand out, one a sensational par three measuring more than 200 metres and dropping 30 metres from tee to green, and the other a double water-carry par four, once described by an American magazine as one of the most difficult holes on earth.

Parts of the Muirhead design have been softened over the years to increase playability for resort guests with some of his more extreme moments dulled down. A constant change of ownership has unfortunately seen course presentation also suffer a dire downturn with fairways and greens no longer up to resort standard and cart paths left virtually derelict. The design however remains compelling and Kooralbyn is a course all serious golfers should tackle at least once.

Royal Queensland Golf Club

Course opened: 1920
Designers: various

Though barely any trace of its original form remains, the current Royal Queensland course is the state's premier classic track. Built on reclaimed riverbank land, the club began as a six hole course in 1920 before extending to 18 holes the following year. In 1926 visiting designer Alister MacKenzie suggested improvements to the greens and bunkers and, though initially implemented, these suggestions have been lost during the club's tumultuous history.

The most significant hardship endured by members came in 1981 when the Queensland Government built the Gateway Bridge across the Brisbane River. The bridge sliced through the Royal Queensland layout, forcing radical changes to the configuration of the back nine. Despite the dramatic vista change, the club has continued to prosper with the holes played towards, under and away from the bridge actually among the best on the course.

Royal Queensland remains an excellent test and worthy championship venue with a number of wonderful driving holes and small, elevated greens with subtle contours and quick surfaces receptive to only the most precise approach shots.

The seemingly gentle 14th is a standout and rated by Australian legend Norman Non Nida as one of the best short par threes in the country. The tiny green is surrounded at the front and side by tight bunkering and by a rough covered bank through the back. With the wind generally whipping across the hole, correct club selection is vital as recovery after an errant tee shot if always difficult.

Robina Woods Golf Course

Course opened: 1989
Designers: Graham Marsh, Ross Watson

Situated within 65 hectares of undulating woodlands Robina Woods is one of the most popular and picturesque public access golf courses in south-east Queensland. With holes built through natural forests of towering eucalypts and full of native wildlife, the course is a peaceful digression from the hustle and bustle of a busy Gold Coast, only minutes away.

'Robina Woods is not big on power but big on thoughtful controlled play. It is tight in places, but it is its beauty that is most memorable.'

Ross Watson

The front nine is played mostly through natural wooded gullies with plenty of dramatic elevation change; the back nine starts on a flatter and less interesting reclaimed floodplain, then heads back into the elevated gully terrain for the scenic and stirring climax.

The pick of the front nine is the downhill left sweeping 6th hole, which, like a number of early holes, favours the player who can hit a strong draw. The closing stretch is particularly impressive with the par five 18th the clear signature hole. Played from a spectacular elevated tee, the final fairway incorporates three lakes as it heads towards an attractive green set beneath the grand multi-level clubhouse.

SOUTH AUSTRALIA

In comparison to the other Australian mainland states, South Australia is a golfing minnow. Despite its diversity of destinations and landscapes, the quality golf revolves around a small number of classic courses close to the Adelaide shoreline.

The game was introduced to the state through the Royal Adelaide Golf Club, which was born a year after Royal Melbourne and formed part of the inaugural council of the Australian Golf Union. Founded near Glenelg, the club moved to Seaton in 1904, and in the process unearthed the Adelaide equivalent of the Melbourne Sandbelt. Though its reddish colour and texture differs from the pristine soft sand of Melbourne, the net effect of building and maintaining quality golf remains the same. Drainage is excellent and the climate ideal for providing the best possible playing surfaces year round.

It took two decades, but by the close of the 1920s, the city's big four—Royal Adelaide, Kooyonga, The Grange and Glenelg—had all found permanent homes along this sandy tract. They immediately established themselves as the state's elite and have experienced very little opposition since, with Royal Adelaide and Kooyonga the clear standouts. Except for Kooyonga, each has undergone drastic restorations over the years.

Throughout the rest of the city and state, the pickings for good golf are extremely lean, despite the seemingly natural attributes of nearby peninsulas and valleys. The most obvious growth region, the Fleurieu Peninsula an hour south of Adelaide, did provide a promising glimpse of potential with the opening of the ambitious Links at Lady Bay development. Totally raw with elements of traditional links golf, the course is unquestionably the best modern track in South Australia.

The state's south-east and Riverland regions are home to a series of attractive country courses such as Mount Gambier, Naracoorte, Berri and Millicent. These courses make a nice golf trip but, to be truthful, all the courses outside the Adelaide Sandbelt together are not worth as much as your next round at Royal Adelaide or Kooyonga.

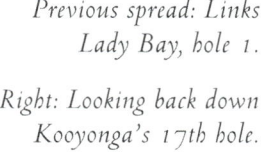

Previous spread: Links Lady Bay, hole 1.

Right: Looking back down Kooyonga's 17th hole.

Kooyonga Golf Club

Course opened: 1922
Designer: H.L. Rymill

The Kooyonga Golf Club was founded when a 1922 train strike forced South Australian golf pioneer, H.L. 'Cargie' Rymill, to take a tram to his home club at Royal Adelaide. During the fateful trip he noticed that a stretch of undulating swampland and sandhills, known as May's Paddock, was for sale. Inspecting the site and realising its potential for great golf, he conceived Kooyonga and immediately acquired the land. Within a few months, the first nine holes were open and by June 1924 a full 18, designed by Rymill himself, were ready for play.

Not formally trained as a golf designer, Rymill was a MacKenzie disciple and carried a copy of his bible, the MacKenzie guide to golf architecture, throughout the Kooyonga project. During the 1990s, this precious relic was returned to the club, complete with highlighted passages and legible Rymill inscriptions on the strategy of his holes as well as the odd snide remark about Royal Adelaide colleagues.

Though raw sandhills dominated the site Rymill first discovered, his design was complemented with grand plantings of native and imported trees which have grown to dominate the landscape. His initial routing remains essentially unchanged, with the most intriguing aspect being the configuration of holes to include back-to-back opening par fives and consecutive par threes on the back nine. He was clearly a man who believed great design could be unconventional.

More conventional, however, is the brilliant use of the land's natural elevation change. Although relatively short, with no par fours over 400 metres and two reachable par fives, the course still provides a stern examination of your skills, largely thanks to the sloping, tight tree-lined fairways and small firm greens.

Kooyonga's unconventional start includes the terrific par five 2nd hole.

Notable course alterations include the building of a pond at the front of the 17th green during the 1980s, and the recent strengthening of the par three 15th when an adjacent property was purchased to allow consulting architects Newton, Grant and Spencer to rebuild and extend the hole. The highlights of the design are the beautiful par five 2nd hole, the two excellent par threes at the 7th and 14th, and the 4th, 8th, 10th and 12th which are all fine par fours with plenty of natural fairway movement.

As a regular tournament venue the club keeps pace with the prodigious professional game by making substantial changes to the course setup during major events. Unable to add much length, fairways are instead narrowed and the severity of the surrounding rough increased to test the modern players. Gary Player once slaughtered par here with two rounds of 62 during the 1965 Australian Open, and the club remains determined to prevent a repeat performance.

Fortunately, away from professional tournaments, members continue to enjoy their traditional setup, with a strategic rather than penal examination and the surrounding trees brought back into play. The fact that today's Kooyonga, with minor upgrades and modifications aside, varies only slightly from the original design, is a fitting tribute to an exceptional man who worked frantically to build a wonderful golf club.

The Links Lady Bay

Course opened: 1998
Designers: Graeme Grant, John Spencer, Jack Newton

The driving force behind the ambitious Links Lady Bay project was a local dairy farmer who sought to create a quality golf experience in an effort to sell real estate on the developing Fleurieu Peninsula, an hour south of Adelaide.

Designed as a traditional links, the course was built by Melbourne superintendent Graeme Grant, who started with his bulldozer at the first tee and did not finish until all 18 holes had been shaped. The eager designer worked sunrise to sunset on what he clearly considered a once in a lifetime piece of land within fertile coastal sand dunes that overlooked the glorious Peninsula coastline.

What Grant and co-designers John Spencer and Jack Newton were able to build is significant considering a limited budget and the ferocious winds that wreaked havoc on the exposed site during construction. At one stage, the developer had to employ nearby schoolchildren to hand plant veldt grass on the dunes besides the 17th green to prevent the sand from blowing away and exposing the freshly laid green. Golfers can expect these same fierce winds to accompany them as they battle their way around the course.

The terrain was well suited to the links concept, with the fairways built out of tumbling sandhills and lined by tall strands of native grasses. Greens are large and beautifully contoured, with superb bentgrass surfaces that roll as true as any celebrated private club in Adelaide. The bunkering was left deliberately wild, which is consistent with the rugged site and helps give the course its timeless and natural appearance.

A brilliant opening tee shot sets the tone for the day with the first hole bending through the dunes towards a green nestled in a hollow and surrounded by large mounds. It's a great start to the round and one of the most attractive holes on the course. The short par four 4th hole is another on the front nine worthy of mention, with its remarkable L-shaped green causing all sorts of headaches for those who misjudge the approach shot.

Bending at almost right angles, the 4th green at Lady Bay is one of South Australia's more 'interesting' targets.

The tricky short four 10th and long par three 17th are the highlights of a back nine which is split by a large ridge running through the site. The long 12th is another classic links hole played through a chute of sand, usually into the stiff south-easterly wind, towards a huge green almost 30 metres long. From the 13th the course heads inland over the hill, with the next four holes played through a valley surrounded by farmland. This less interesting land was used for golf to maximise the residential allotments and ensure each home site overlooked course and coastline. The best outlook though is saved for those on the 17th tee as the hole cuts back across the ridge towards the main site with stunning views of the distant sea.

The Links may not quite reach the dizzy heights of its big budget contemporaries, but is an outstanding experience and clearly South Australia's finest modern golf course.

The Grange Golf Club, West Course
Course opened: 1956
Designer: Vern Morcom

With golf clubs at Kooyonga, Royal Adelaide and Glenelg establishing an elite Adelaide Sandbelt, a small group of passionate golfers, mostly from working class backgrounds, got together in 1926 to form the city's final 'big four' club, The Grange. They initially leased a 120-acre parcel of small reddish sand mounds known as 'The Pinery' which were covered in shrubs and littered with pine trees. The site was perfectly situated just a few hundred metres from Royal Adelaide and less than a kilometre from the banks of the Port River.

By the 1950s the club had enjoyed rapid growth and, with a thriving membership and modern clubhouse, decided to commission Victorian Vern Morcom to consult on major changes to the existing course. His task was to toughen up the test, and over a period of nine years he built eighteen new tees, seventeen new greens and shaped considerable areas of new fairway. The full upgrade was completed in 1965. During these development years the club was also busy securing the use of an adjacent parcel of land, which in 1967 opened as the East Course, also designed by Morcom.

The Grange has Adelaide's most distinctive parkland feel, with holes defined by rows of tall pines. The slightly superior West Course includes a series of excellent closing par fours, the 17th especially enjoyable as it beautifully follows the natural movement of the land and sweeps through a chute of pines, first to the right, and then slightly uphill.

Although also an excellent track, the East Course is best remembered as the venue of Greg Norman's first professional title, the 1976 West Lakes Classic.

The Grange Golf Club, West Course.

Glenelg Golf Club
Course opened: 1927
Designers: Vern Morcom (1950), Neil Crafter, Bob Touhy

Originally founded in 1926, today's Glenelg golf course was designed by Vern Morcom after the club's land was redistributed in 1946 as part of the Adelaide airport project. The holes were initially laid out through an undulating forest of tall pines, which decades of overzealous committees 'complemented' with scores of additional trees.

In 1998, with the site badly overplanted, the club embarked on a radical restoration program with the aim of returning the site to its predominantly pine tree character, and also re-establishing an open links-like appearance on the more exposed areas of the course.

Consultants Neil Crafter and Bob Touhy oversaw the removal of the introduced plants and also modernised the layout by adding a number of championship tees and reconfiguring almost half the holes. They also completely rebuilt each of the bunkers with revetted faces, the first such undertaking of its kind in Australia.

Of the new holes, the short par four 13th is the most attractive, while the long sweeping par four 2nd remains the pick of the originals. The large Pine Hill, which dominates the club's entrance, is still a prominent feature on a number of the better driving holes, including the semi-blind tee shot on the 9th and the steep uphill drive through the trees on the 10th.

Although the restoration has been positive, the contrasting parkland and linksland styles do leave the layout slightly incoherent. Nonetheless, Glenelg is an extremely enjoyable golf course with plenty of interesting holes, and is well worth a look for any golfer visiting South Australia.

RATINGS

Aside from being totally subjective and highly contentious, golf ranking lists are merely an indication of the perceived standard of a golf course or golf hole. None can possibly provide an accurate or 'official' rank of quality because of the many outside variables and the fact that a definitive description of great golf still does not exist. Golf courses are all different and every golfer, including those who judge, takes something unique away from each round they play. Some look to pristine perfection and an artificial shape, others seek uncomplicated golf in natural surrounds that can thrill with pure beauty. Some prefer parkland, others linksland, heathland, or resort style.

Most rating systems are based on the methodology of assigning numeric values to the elements that typically make up a golf course—its Design, Setting and Conditioning.

Design covers the widest scope and is often split with buzz phrases like 'Shot Values', 'Design Variety' and 'Memorability' forming their own sub-categories. This seems unduly technical, however, as judging a design should subliminally include them all. Setting is again quite broad and as well as covering the usual categories of the ambience and aesthetics of a site, it should also consider how the holes are set within the land's natural features; in other words, what works visually both inside and outside the design. The final and most contentious area of analysis is course conditioning or presentation, the rating's grey area.

'Any man who dreams that the golf course he has laid out will meet with universal approval is doomed to disappointment.'

Garden G. Smith,
The World of Golf, 1898

The par five 17th hole at the underrated but incredible Grand Golf Club.

Unfortunately, how a course is groomed is often given as much importance as how the holes are actually designed and built. In most cases, judges only see the courses once or twice and as a result, typical conditioning cannot be accurately assessed. While true that over time one can develop an understanding of how a golf course generally plays, if too rigid in this assessment, then changes in greenkeeping practices or course renovations become meaningless. Therefore, in my view, course conditioning should come a very distant third to design and setting, with course appraisals shifted only slightly up or slightly down if the grooming is outside the scope of what is considered average, a scope that has widened considerably in recent years.

About the only thing ranking lists successfully achieve is the stirring of healthy debate. A broad scale rating system devised to categorise rather than compare the quality of each design is a much clearer and fairer way of analysing the strengths and weaknesses of a golf course. American architect Tom Doak created his famous Doak scale for this very purpose. Assigning each course a score out of ten, his system works best at identifying the quality of a group of golf courses without the burden of having to rank them in sequential order.

Personally, I find an even broader scale of description using basic terminology like 'good', 'very good' and 'outstanding' can work just as well in measuring personal tastes and opinions. Of course, all golfers have their bias, but accepting that each track is essentially 'very good' makes arguing over an actual ranking placement little more than extraneous fun.

Leading classics are a perfect illustration of how difficult and feeble the system can become. Kingston Heath, New South Wales and Royal Adelaide are all outstanding, yet I find them difficult to rank because, if pressed, I'd give the points to Kingston Heath for architecture, to New South Wales for thrills and to Royal Adelaide for pure charm. All are important ingredients. Royal Adelaide and New South Wales have the greater disparity between their best and worst holes but Royal Adelaide has the most original features and New South Wales the most inspired setting. Kingston Heath has the best bunkering and the best par three, Royal Adelaide the best par four, New South Wales the best par five and on it goes.

The only truly accurate rankings, therefore, are an individual's own; the composition of such a list cannot be disputed. Having said this, and although admitting they are mostly futile, rankings do make fascinating reading and give a general 'quality' overview to those who have not seen the full sample. They can also be great fun and given the inevitability of the 'which is best?' question, I have decided to rate what I believe are the finest courses, holes, sites and experiences in Australian golf.

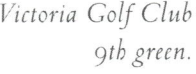

Victoria Golf Club
9th green.

Best Australian Golf Holes

Best Par Threes—Classic

Kingston Heath 15th
Royal Melbourne West 5th
Yarra Yarra 11th
New South Wales 6th
Royal Melbourne East 16th
Woodlands 17th
Newcastle 7th
Kingston Heath 10th
Metropolitan 2nd
Royal Melbourne West 7th
Peninsula North 14th
Kingston Heath 5th
Barwon Heads 13th
New South Wales 11th
Royal Queensland 14th
Royal Melbourne East 4th
National Moonah 17th
Ellerston 2nd
National Ocean 11th
Glades 17th
Links Lady Bay 17th

National Old 7th

Kingston Heath 15th

Best Par Threes—Modern

National Old 7th
Thirteenth Beach 12th
Ellerston 6th
Thirteenth Beach 16th
Kennedy Bay 16th
Capital 8th
The Dunes 17th
National Moonah 5th
Thirteenth Beach 7th
Capital 16th
Joondalup (Quarry) 3rd

Best Set of Par Threes—Classic

Kingston Heath
Yarra Yarra
Royal Melbourne West
Royal Melbourne East
New South Wales

Royal Melbourne West 5th

Best Set of Par Threes—Modern

Thirteenth Beach
Ellerston
Capital
Laguna Quays
The Dunes
National Moonah

Best Par Fours—Classic
(over 340m)

Royal Melbourne West 6th
Royal Melbourne West 17th
Royal Canberra 16th
Commonwealth 16th
Royal Adelaide 11th
New South Wales 15th
Royal Melbourne East 18th
Newcastle 5th
Royal Adelaide 14th
Commonwealth 11th
Yarra Yarra 5th
Kingston Heath 6th
Royal Melbourne West 18th
Metropolitan 5th
Peninsula South 17th
New South Wales 7th
Royal Adelaide 18th
Royal Melbourne East 2nd
Victoria 13th

The Dunes 8th
The Vintage 2nd
Thirteenth Beach 8th
Capricorn New 17th
Capital 6th
Heritage 8th

Royal Melbourne West 10th

Royal Melbourne West 6th

Best Par Fours—Modern
(over 340m)

Ellerston 16th
National Moonah 11th
Kennedy Bay 15th
National Moonah 3rd
Ellerston 7th
Vines Lakes 11th
National Moonah 4th
Ellerston 5th
Capital 17th
Glades 2nd
Laguna Quays 6th
National Moonah 10th

Best Par Fours—Classic
(under 340m)

Royal Adelaide 3rd
Kingston Heath 3rd
Royal Melbourne West 10th
New South Wales 14th
Royal Melbourne East 1st
Woodlands 7th
Kingston Heath 9th
Commonwealth 17th
Victoria 15th
The Lakes 10th
Royal Melbourne East 15th
Woodlands 13th
Royal Melbourne West 3rd
Woodlands 4th
Portsea 13th
Peninsula North 13th

Royal Adelaide 3rd

Best Par Fours—Modern (under 340m)

Pelican Waters 12th
Kennedy Bay 7th
The Dunes 4th
Thirteenth Beach 5th
Glades 16th
The Grand 10th
Kennedy Bay 12th
Pelican Waters 2nd
Ranfurlie 16th
Thirteenth Beach 13th
Hyatt Coolum 5th
Moonah Links 1st
The Vintage 4th
Joondalup (Lake) 2nd
National Ocean 13th
Lakelands 8th
Links Lady Bay 10th

Best Set of Par Fours—Modern

Ellerston
National Moonah
Kennedy Bay
The Dunes
Capital

The Dunes 4th

Pelican Waters 12th

Best Par Fives—Classic

New South Wales 5th
Royal Melbourne West 4th
Kingston Heath 14th
The Lakes 11th
Victoria 9th
Woodlands 15th
Royal Melbourne East 17th
Royal Melbourne West 12th
Kooyonga 2nd
Royal Melbourne East 10th
Peninsula South 8th
Newcastle 10th
Yarra Yarra 9th
Kingston Heath 7th
Peninsula North 15th
Royal Sydney 16th

Best Set of Par Fours—Classic

Royal Melbourne West
Royal Adelaide
Kingston Heath
Commonwealth
Newcastle
New South Wales,
Royal Melbourne East

Kingston Heath 9th

Woodlands 15th

Best Par Fives—Modern

Ellerston 9th
National Moonah 15th
National Moonah 2nd
Ellerston 10th
Capital 7th
National Moonah 7th
Palm Meadows 18th
Thirteenth Beach 6th
The Grand 12th
Ellerston 1st
Hope Island 8th
Kennedy Bay 8th
Thirteenth Beach 4th
The Dunes 12th
Thirteenth Beach 11th
Joondalup (Quarry) 4th
Glades 7th

Hope Island 8th

Best Set of Par Fives—Classic

Kingston Heath
The Lakes
Royal Melbourne West
Victoria
Yarra Yarra

The Lakes 14th

Best Set of Par Fives—Modern

National Moonah
Ellerston
Thirteenth Beach
Hope Island
Kennedy Bay

Ellerston 10th

Hardest Holes

National Ocean 18th
Sanctuary Cove Pines 10th
Ellerston 16th
National Ocean 9th
National Moonah 16th
Moonah Links 18th
Kooralbyn 15th
Ellerston 3rd
Kooralbyn 5th
National Old 3rd
Ellerston 8th
National Old 7th
The Grand 9th
Joondalup (Dune) 4th
Yarra Yarra 11th
Ellerston 15th
Moonah Links 15th

Sanctuary Cove Pines 10th

Most Spectacular Holes

National Old 7th
New South Wales 5th
New South Wales 6th
Royal Melbourne West 4th
Ellerston 16th
National Ocean 1st
New South Wales 14th
National Moonah 11th
Ellerston 7th
Narooma 3rd
Joondalup (Quarry) 3rd
Ellerston 6th
Laguna Quays 13th
Kooralbyn 5th
National Old 17th

Best Opening Hole

Metropolitan
Royal Melbourne East
Portsea
Kingston Heath
Ellerston
The Lakes
Royal Adelaide
Woodlands
Moonah Links
Kennedy Bay
Links Lady Bay
National Moonah

The Lakes 1st

National Old 7th

Best Closing Hole

Royal Melbourne East
Royal Melbourne West
Royal Adelaide
Ellerston
Royal Sydney
Commonwealth
Kingston Heath
National Moonah
Palm Meadows
The Dunes

Commonwealth 16th

Ellerston 18th

Best Opening Stretch (Holes 1–3)

Royal Melbourne East
Metropolitan
National Moonah
Kingston Heath
Royal Adelaide
Ellerston
Royal Melbourne West

Best Closing Stretch (Holes 16–18)

Royal Melbourne East
Commonwealth
Royal Melbourne West

Kingston Heath
Ellerston
National Moonah
Metropolitan

Best Consecutive Holes (Any Three)

Royal Melbourne West 4–6
New South Wales 5–7
Royal Melbourne East 16–18
Ellerston 5–7
Newcastle 5–7
Kingston Heath 14–16
Royal Melbourne East 1–3
Commonwealth 16–18
New South Wales 13–15
Capital 6–8
Peninsula North 12–14

Hardest Closing Stretch (Holes 16–18)

Moonah Links
National Moonah
Sanctuary Lakes
The Australian
National Ocean

National Moonah 2nd

Best Australian Golf Courses

Best Private Course—Classic

Royal Melbourne West
Kingston Heath
New South Wales
Royal Adelaide
Royal Melbourne East
Victoria
Metropolitan
Commonwealth
Woodlands
Royal Sydney

Royal Melbourne West 7th

Best Private Course—Modern

Ellerston
National Moonah
Capital
National Old
The Grand
Ranfurlie
Terrey Hills
National Ocean
Heritage

The Capital 18th

Best Non-Member Access

Kennedy Bay
Newcastle
The Dunes
Thirteenth Beach
Laguna Quays
Brookwater
Portsea
The Vintage
Glades
Hope Island
Joondalup

Brookwater 13th

Hardest Courses

Ellerston
Moonah Links
National Ocean
National Moonah
Capital
Sanctuary Cove Pines
Joondalup
Kooralbyn
Paradise Palms
National Old

Moonah Links 4th

Meanest Back Tees

Moonah Links
Royal Adelaide
Kooralbyn
National Moonah
Brookwater
Paradise Palms

Moonah Links 3rd

Best Redesign/Restoration

Peninsula North
The Lakes
The Australian
Portsea
Concord

Best Inland Course

Ellerston
Royal Canberra
Brookwater
The Vintage
Heritage

The Vintage

Best Coastal Course

New South Wales
National Moonah
Kennedy Bay
Newcastle
Thirteenth Beach, Portsea

New South Wales 7th

Best Golf Sites

Royal Melbourne
New South Wales
Royal Adelaide
National Moonah/Ocean
Kingston Heath
Thirteenth Beach
Kooyonga
Peninsula North
The Dunes
Newcastle
Portsea

National Ocean 1st

Best Transformation: Bad Land, Great Result

Capital
Metropolitan
Glades
Hope Island
Pelican Waters

Most Attractive Setting

Royal Melbourne
Metropolitan
Bonville
Royal Canberra
Kingston Heath
Ellerston
Kooyonga
Royal Adelaide
Brookwater
The Grand
Laguna Quays
Yarra Yarra

Most Dramatic Setting

New South Wales
National Old
National Moonah/Ocean
Royal Melbourne
Thirteenth Beach
Ellerston
Joondalup
Laguna Quays
Brookwater
Secret Harbour

National Moonah 11th

Best Views

New South Wales
National Old
National Moonah/Ocean
Laguna Quays
Ellerston

New South Wales 5th

Best Bunkering—Classic

Kingston Heath
Royal Melbourne
Victoria
Commonwealth
Woodlands
Yarra Yarra

Bonville 17h

Best Bunkering—Modern

Ellerston
National Moonah
Thirteenth Beach
Brookwater
Kennedy Bay
The Dunes

National Moonah 10th

Ellerston 9th

Best Greens—Classic

Royal Melbourne
Kingston Heath
Yarra Yarra
Victoria
Woodlands
Commonwealth
Royal Canberra
Metropolitan
Kooyonga
Royal Adelaide
Concord

Best Conditioned Courses—Modern

Ellerston
Capital
Meadow Springs
Laguna Quays
The Grand
Glades
The Dunes
(Note: this refers to the best conditioned courses during the research for this book, which may not necessarily reflect year-round conditioning.)

Capital 7th

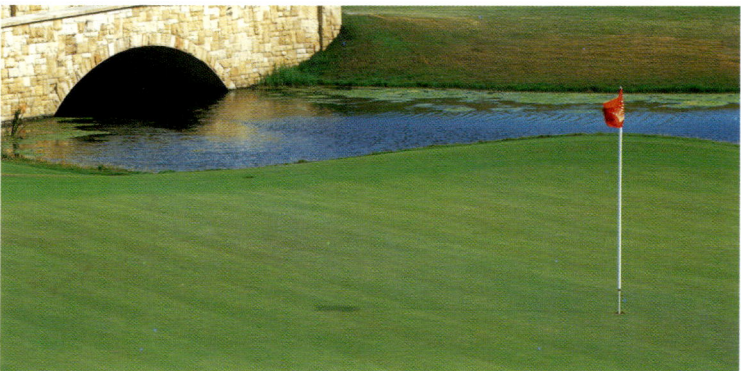

Best Greens—Modern

Ellerston
National Moonah
Capital
Kennedy Bay
Glades
Thirteenth Beach
The Grand
Vines Lakes
The Dunes
Terrey Hills
Links Lady Bay
Hope Island

Best Conditioned Courses—Classic

Metropolitan
Kingston Heath
Royal Melbourne
Royal Sydney
Woodlands
Yarra Yarra
Royal Queensland
Royal Canberra
(Note: this refers to the best conditioned courses during the research for this book, which may not necessarily reflect year-round conditioning.)

ACKNOWLEDGMENTS

This book would not have been possible without the support of the Australian golf industry, and I am most thankful for the assistance received from all the Managers, Secretaries, Presidents, Professionals, Superintendents and office staff that I came in contact with throughout the country.

A deep appreciation is especially extended to Australia's private golf clubs for granting me the privilege of access to their courses and historical literature. In particular, I would like to acknowledge Michael Armstrong, Rob Ashes, Ross Bishop, David Burton, Graham Christian, Adrian Edgar, Bill Francis, Doug Jacka, Shawn Mahoney, Ken Manders, Bruce Miller, Paul Rak, Bill Richardson, Gary Richardson, Kingsley Robinson, Allan Shorland, Peter Stackpole, Lindsay Stade, Cameron Wade, Michael Waring, Don Will and Michael Williams for their assistance.

I am also immensely indebted to Lloyd Williams and Ishan Ratnam at Capital Golf Club, and Kerry Packer, Tony Clark and the whole team at Ellerston, and thank them for opening their gates and permitting me the joy of sharing their tremendous bounties with a curious golfing public.

Special acknowledgment is also extended to the various designers and developers who generously contributed their thoughts and shared their passions: Duncan Andrews, Tony Cashmore, Michael Clayton, Michael Coate, Neil Crafter, Bob Harrison, Mike Hill, Greg Norman, Ross Perrett, Peter Thomson, Ross Watson and Michael Wolveridge.

To friends and colleagues Selwyn Berg, Paul Daley, Brendan James, Tom Ramsey and David Scaletti I thank you all for your help and wisdom throughout this journey.

On a personal note, I wish to extend a special thanks to Bob Harrison for his incredible generosity and friendship throughout and his extraordinary willingness to support the project from day one. My sincerest gratitude also to Ian Baker-Finch for his incisive foreword and for the memories of 36 wonderful holes at The National.

Finally, and most importantly, my love and thanks to Persia and Indy for putting the bogeys into perspective, to Emma for her help and brutal honesty and to Leeanne for the sacrifices and for patiently putting up with my single-mindedness.

Brookwater Golf Club

INDEX

For Tress Oliver and Greg Norman,
who introduced me to the game of golf and then inspired me to pursue it.

First published in Australia in 2003 by
New Holland Publishers (Australia) Pty Ltd
Sydney • Auckland • London • Cape Town

14 Aquatic Drive Frenchs Forest NSW 2086 Australia
218 Lake Road Northcote Auckland New Zealand
86 Edgware Road London W2 2EA United Kingdom
80 McKenzie Street Cape Town 8001 South Africa

National Library of Australia Cataloguing-in-Publication Data:

    Oliver, Darius.
    Australia's finest golf courses.

    Includes index.
    ISBN 1 86436 789 X.

    1. Golf courses — Australia. I. Title.

    796.3520994

Publishing Manager: Anouska Good
Project Editors: Sophie Church and Claire de Medici
Copy Editor: saso content and design
Designer: Karlman Roper
Production Manager: Linda Bottari
Reproduction: Colourscan
Printer: Kyodo

10 9 8 7 6 5 4 3 2 1